# THE VIETNAMESE
# ENTREPRENEURS
# IN THE U.S.A.

## THE FIRST DECADE

## JOHN KONG LEBA, M.B.A., Ph.D.

WITH:

JOHN H. LEBA, B.B.A., M.Sc.
ANTHONY T. LEBA, B.M.E., M.B.A.

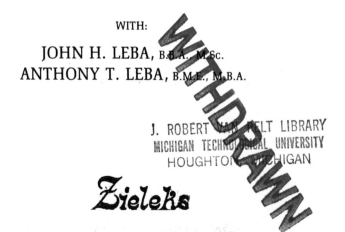

Zieleks

*Kính dâng hương hồn*
*Song Thân*
**L.B.K.**

Abstract of the Dissertation

# THE VIETNAMESE ENTREPRENEURS
# IN THE U.S.A.
The First Decade (1975-1985)

By
John K. Leba

Doctor of Philosophy in Business Administration
California Coast University
Santa Ana, California
1985

In the aftermath of the Vietnam War with the extinction of the Republic of Vietnam as a nation, the initial contingents comprising some 150,000 Indochinese (among whom over 125,000 were Vietnamese) were hastily and panic-strickenly transported by U.S. military planes and naval vessels out of the besieged conclave of Saigon and its outskirts to wherever there was safety from communist merciless atrocities and reprisals.

Those refugees came to the new land to add another ethnic group to the gigantic melting-pot of racial mixture in existence in this nation for already so many years. The newcomers were confronted with countless hardships since the first days setting foot on this soil, but thanks to their generous and hospitable American hosts, after the first decade of trials, efforts and patience, they have found new lives in their adopted homeland — the United States of America.

The Vietnamese refugee-immigrants, like their predecessors of other ethnic stocks, want to live decently, and furthermore, they also want to be successful in this land of opportunity. According to the latest report, the current Vietnamese population in the U.S. is approximately 590,000 people.

The author's intention, as presented in Chapter 1 of this study, aims at offering the readers some brief introductory remarks on the historical events, geographical features, social and cultural traits of Vietnam. This is then followed by a review of and some insight into the Vietnam War and its immediate consequences as expressed in Chapter 2.

The subsequent chapter serves as a synopsis to the dissertation by featuring ten representative cases depicting the various business activities professed by the Vietnamese newcomers. In all of these instances, the author has disguised companies, used fictitious names and taken precautions to preserve the confidential nature and anonymity of those referred to. Similarities and familiarities may occur, and this merely demonstrates the universality of cases and problems in the numerous Vietnamese communities recently formed in the United States.

Through observations, surveys, documentations and researches, the author concludes that pinpointing a problem is sometimes easy, but doing something about it is highly complex. The information collected is almost always interesting and useful, but it often heightens his desire to make suggestions to his compatriots to remedy the defects.

Thus, in Chapters 4 and 5, helpful tips and hints are offered, because the author strongly believes that the Vietnamese-American entrepreneurs can always improve their businesses efficiently, change their outmoded perceptions, attitudes and understandings so as to adapt themselves to current circumstances. Each of them should seek a course of action that represents the best solution to his problem. Each is confronted with a chance to do the right, ethical, moral and businesslike thing in order to acquire the most rewarding results.

Many people don't mind working hard to achieve success, but only hard work does not necessarily bring about success. It is certainly an ingredient of success, but it is not the only ingredient. The successful individual must master the rules of success, or better still if the conclusive advice is phrased as follows: "To be successful in this country, the entrepreneur must effectively apply the right American methods."

The present work is just the first stepping stone on the long unending entrepreneurial road for the Vietnamese-American businesspeople to be aware of their actual situations. The author appeals to others of his country-fellows to continue their contribution in some way or other to help enrich the knowledge of modern business administration among the Vietnamese residents in the U.S.A.

## ACKNOWLEDGEMENT

In June, 1983, the candidate submitted his dissertation proposal to Prof. Philip S. Borden, Dean, School of Administration and Management, California Coast University, and on July 22, 1983, he received the official letter informing him of the Graduate Review Committee's approval of the proposal with a personal handwritten note from Prof. Borden which says, "We like the dissertation proposal which promises (1) an important study which will be valuable beyond the academic requirements, (2) strong personal involvement and interest by the author, and (3) a significant and well stated research question to be answered."

Needless to say, the message brought great inspiration and stimulation to the candidate, who is currently 60 years old, to keep on doing research work during these two past years in spite of the ordeal of a triple bypass surgical operation that he had to go through in October, 1983. The author feels that in manifesting his ultimate efforts in completing successfully the various preceding phases in fulfillment of the entire academic requirements since enrollment in the program in 1981 as well as in acquiring the credit hours accumulated in numerous courses offered by other universities, colleges and professional institutes, he not only gained additional knowledge for his personal benefits, but also set a good example to the thousands of younger compatriots — students and youths — to demonstrate special keenness in improving their academic and technological backgrounds whenever and wherever circumstances permit.

This study is a work of inspiration and involvement rather than of profound research. The author hopes it will prove useful to a wide variety of readers, Vietnamese and American. The modest research work may be helpful to students in "case" courses who need some references to concepts.

The author gratefully acknowledges the encouragement instilled upon him by Dr. Philip S. Borden, his Dean and Field Advisor, during these past years. Without such encouraging and inspirational counsels, he might have abandoned the final efforts in completing the dissertation. A special word of appreciation is also extended to the candidate's two sons: John, Jr. (B.B.A., Iona College, M.Sc., University of Houston) and Anthony (B.M.E., M.B.A., University of Houston) for having contributed their perception and viewpoints to the author's endeavors while drafting this work. During his lifetime, as father and educator, he has constantly offered advice and motivation to them, but in the course of the past four years, they were the ones who brought inspiration to him.

The candidate also wishes to express special thanks to his brother, Francis K. Leba, for helping with bilingual translations of English and Vietnamese documents, while Norma Zimpel and Luu Ngoc Bich helped in gathering research materials from great numbers of books, newspapers, magazines, reports and library documentations.

And finally the candidate wishes to thank the University of Houston's libraries at the University Park and at the Clear Lake Campus for use of their facilities for much of the research in completing this dissertation.

J.K.L.

# TABLE OF CONTENTS

## APPENDIXES

*xiv*

TABLE

PAGE

## LIST OF FIGURES

## MAP

Chapter 1

## INTRODUCTION TO THE SELECTED PROBLEM

- Introductory Remarks

- Historical Highlights

- Courage and Morale

- Cultural Influences

- Influences of the Social Structure

Chapter 1

## INTRODUCTION TO
## THE SELECTED PROBLEM

**Introductory Remarks**

In order to survive, especially for hundreds of thousands of newcomers to a strange land where most of the environments are entirely new in all respects, they must solve some basic problems: they must earn their living by having to procure adequate food, clothing, and shelter. Beyond these needs, they also share a common desire, which is to form their own ethnic communities in which they can enjoy their traditional cultural heritage. Because of this demand, a new social group has come into existence to add its flavor to the colossal melting pot of racial groups in this land of Freedom and Justice.

How these men and women will behave themselves and with other groups marks the beginning of a new era - the first decade - of the Vietnamese newcomers to the United States of America.

As time passes by, these people will gradually assimilate th mselves into the new American mainstream of life. The gene ration of the adults will certainly show considerable resista nce to the new ways of life on the American continent, but futu re generations will consciously or unconsciously mingle t hemselves with the cultures of their American brothers. The essential goal now is to preserve as much Vietnamese heritage as possible among this new ethnic group in the U.S.A. The current modest study is only a preliminary effort to highlight the gist of a great problem of the residents of Vietnamese ancestry as well as to the people of other racial stocks to constantly keep this significant issue in their minds and hearts. Vietnamese culture is and will be contributing a great asset to the overall multifaceted culture in this great nation.

The Vietnamese refugee-immigrants have brought along with them a particular family system, a quite different social structure, and other ethnic particularities. However, they have to adjust to the climate and geography of the region where they are to settle down to set up their new homes. They will have different ways of solving some of the basic problems: sometimes by their traditional methods sometimes by "new" methods adopted or learned in their second homeland.

**Basic Backgrounds.**

In order to understand the principal traits and characteristics of the Vietnamese people, the reader must have some notion of at least the historical, social and cultural backgrounds of this heroic and proud race. He will then be able to share the deep nostalgia that each Vietnamese feels as the latter has been obliged to leave his Fatherland which fell into the astrocious communistic rulers' hands. Through understanding the close attachment and affection that the Vietnamese individual cherishes for his homeland, the reader can then draw from this the conclusion as to how inhuman and barbarous the Marxist doctrine imposes on mankind. Throughout the past centuries, having had to experience wars, natural calamities, and famines, the Vietnamese people had always clung to their homeland. But with the communistic totalitarian yoke weighing heavily upon their shoulders, they

have to flee for their lives in search of freedom for themselves
and their descendants just as millions of other freedom-loving
people of East Europe have done so in recent years.

Having to accept self-imposed exile from the Fatherland,
the Vietnamese refugee-immigrants nourish in their souls a
lingering anxiety and concern for their future and that of their
progenies. They felt lost in a strange land. At first, they
thought they would be completely strange and unfamiliar with
the new life, new customs, language barrier, and numerous
other major problems. Fortunately, they have been welcomed
warmly by very friendly and hospitable Americans in the
various regions all over this extensive country. Enjoying the
spontaneous assistance of the local people, the newcomers
have felt great comfort and consolation, and above all,
encouragement to start their new lives. The American
benefactors can be assured of the profound gratitude of these
newcomers. The Samaritan attitude demonstrated by those
generous and magnanimous hosts will be forever engraved in
the hearts of all those who benefitted by their kindly gestures.

Realizing some of the immediate problems that
Vietnamese new entrepreneurs have confronted these past
years in the United States, the author - through observations,
surveys and researches - tries to contribute his efforts in
working out some solutions as well as offering constructive
suggestions and recommendations in a casual and intimate
style.

Through the ten representative case studies in Chapter
Three of this work, the writer hopes to tackle the problems in
some key areas. Thus, it is his sincere hope that the successes
and failures encountered by the Vietnamese-American
entrepreneurs during the past decade can serve as useful and

practical lessons to those who are on the verge of going into business. No lesson is as valuable and costly as experience. If all the men and women who face complex and unstructured problems in their business undertakings can make use of this unpretentious study, the author feels he has already been amply rewarded.

## HISTORICAL HIGHLIGHTS

Like all other people on the surface of the earth, the Vietnamese must deal with the same basic problems: they must find food, clothing and shelter. Beyond this, they also strived to build a social group. In so doing they developed a culture, a family system, a government, and other forms of organization while adjusting to external forces such as the climate, geography and foreign intrusions of their nation. Ultimately, their lives will form a pattern socio-cultural group that we call, in this case, "Vietnamese".

No definite date has been found regarding the organization of the Vietnamese society, but according to some authoritative historians, the history of Vietnam began in about the year 2897 B.C. with the establishment of the Hong Bang dynasty which lasted till the year 258 B.C. [1]

The nation of Vietnam, through its long history of nearly five thousand years, had undergone so many changes, especially in several periods of time when it was subjugated by China, its powerful northern neighbor. In the meantime the nation continued to evolve while its territory also expanded southward to the Cape of Ca-Mau. Changes even occurred after the first Westerners (Portuguese, Spaniards and Dutch) arrived in Central Vietnam (A.D. 1614) and North Vietnam (A.D. 1637). [2]

---

[1]*Tran Trong Kim, "Viet-Nam Su Luoc" (Outline of the History of Vietnam), Dept. of Education, Republic of Vietnam, Saigon, 1971, vol. I, p. 3.*
[2]*Ibid.*

In order to have a better understanding of the Vietnamese people, it is the belief of the candidate that the reader should be familiar with the highlights of the History of Vietnam as well as the cultural and social background of the Vietnamese people. The people of the Western world, especially those of France and the U.S.A., during the recent four decades, had been involved in Vietnam. Inevitably, some other nations as well, in one way or another, will find themselves tied to the destiny of that particular "remote" country - Vietnam. The people of the world should know more of one another in a more sophisticated manner through education and cultural exchanges at a non-war time. A more sharply-focused picture of the Vietnamese newcomers to the U.S.A. and other free countries is helpful in building better relationship between the hosts and the new "guests", by bringing the former closer to the Vietnamese reality.

The reader does not have to be an expert about Vietnam, but he should at least be knowledgeable of the general history and geography of that nation which was for a number of years tied to the political scenarios of the U.S.A.. The great frustration to the candidate was that quite a few American intellectuals had been offered a wrong or distorted picture of the Republic of Vietnam under a democratic regime, by the very powerful and influential media in this country. There were also numerous writers and commentators who claimed themselves to be experts, professionals and authorities on Vietnam issues, while in reality most of them spent only one or two years reading about that country. Who would not be frustrated and "annoyed by the absurdities presented in all seriousness, by the misquotations offered as documentation, by the outright violence of the diatribes, by the quivering emotionalism of the unsubstantiated charges, and the sheer authoritarianism of allegations stated as facts"? [3]

[3]John J. O'Connor, "A Chaplain Looks at Vietnam," The World Publishing Co., Cleveland, 1968, p. xiii. (Currently the Rev. O'Connor is Cardinal and Archbishop of New York.)

The following highlights of the History of Vietnam will enable the reader to have a general understanding of the main events that occurred during the past 50 centuries in that relatively small nation (roughly the size of California).

## TABLE OF EVENTS *

2897-258 B.C.
Legendary period, the Hong Bang dynasty. King Lac Long became the first ruler. The name of the nation was then called Van-Lang.

257-207 B.C.
An Duong Vuong founded the Thuc dynasty and changed the name of the nation to Au-Lac.

208 B.C.
Trieu Da, a Chinese general, conquered Au-Lac in the northern mountains of Vietnam, established a capital, and proclaimed himself emperor of "Nam Viet" (Southern Viet).

207-111 B.C.
Trieu Da overthrew the Thuc dynasty and founded the Trieu dynasty. The country was named Nam Viet.

111 B.C. - A.D. 39
Han dynasty (of China) expanded and incorporated Nam Viet into the Chinese empire as the province of Giao Chi. Introduction of Chinese culture. Beginning of over 1000 years of Chinese domination in Vietnam.

A.D. 40-43
Trung sisters (Trung Trac and Trung Nhi) led a major insurrection against the Chinese and set up an independent

*Based on data taken from Tran Trong Kim, "Outline of the History of Vietnam" (Viet-Nam Su Luoc), Vol. I & II, Dept. of Education, Republic of Vietnam, 1971.*

state.

**A.D. 43-544**
Second domination by the Chinese.

**222-280**
In China the opening era of the Wu (Ngo) dynasty. This was the era of the Three Kingdoms in China.

**400**
Foundation of Indrapura, the capital of Champa (Central Vietnam today).

**265-420**
The Tan dynasty came to power in China.

**420-588**
China was partitioned into South under the Tong (Sung) dynasty and North under the Nguy dynasty.

**542-547**
Ly Bon revolted against the Chinese, founded the Kingdom of Yen-Xuan whose capital was Long-Bien, and proclaimed himself Emperor (544). He was assassinated in 547 and his kingdom was conquered by China.

**589**
Ly Xuan unsuccessfully revolted against the Chinese.

**602-939**
Ly Phat Tu failed to overthrow the Chinese. The Vietnamese peasants suffered tremendously during the Chinese domination. The third time, Vietnam was under Chinese yoke.

679

The Tan dynasty (618-907) of China declared Giao-Chi (a former name for Vietnam) a Protectorate General and renamed it An Nam, meaning "Pacified Southern Province", with TONG BINH (Hanoi) as its capital. Chinese culture flourished.

820

The Vietnamese founded their own Buddhist sect: Thien-Vo-Ngon-Thong in Vietnam.

875

The Cham dynasty of Indrapura; the most prosperous period of Cham arts. Buddhism and Taoism were recognized as the official religions in Vietnam.

938

Ngo Quyen drove the Chinese out of Vietnam and founded the Ngo dynasty.

946

Vietnam regained her political independence from foreign invaders. However, it was deeply influenced by Chinese culture.

972

Vietnam was recognized as an independent state by China.

980

The Dinh dynasty came to power.

991

The beginning era of the (Early) Le dynasty.

**922**

Vietnamese military expedition was being sent to the Kingdom of Champa (Central Vietnam) in its efforts to expand the empire southward.

**1009-1225**

The Ly dynasty. The Emperor performed three roles:
  1.- Divine ruler of the nation.
  2.- Absolute monarch.
  3.- Religious Head communicating with Heaven.

The Mandarinate (high ranking administrative body) was introduced, comprising six ministries: 1. manpower, 2. finance, 3. rites, 4. justice, 5. armed forces, and 6. public works.

**1069**

Emperor Ly Thanh Tong, the third Emperor of the Ly dynasty, renamed the nation and called it Dai-Viet (Great Viet). Buddhism was made state religion. Confucianism and Taoism were also encouraged.

**1075-1077**

Ly Thuong Kiet led Vietnamese armies to attack China where he inflicted great defeats on the Chinese forces of the Sung dynasty.

**1076**

National Academy for madarins' sons was founded in Hanoi by King Ly Nhan-Ton.

**1094**

Demarcation of the boundary line between the two countries: China and Vietnam.

**1174**

The Chinese Emperor recognized Ly Anh-Tong as ruler of An-Nam.

**1225-1400**

The Tran dynasty. The Kingdom of Champa was invaded by Viet-Nam. Confucianism took over the prevailing role of Buddhism as a national cult with emphasis on philosophy and literature. Sai Thung, an arrogant Mongol envoy, visited An-Nam paving the way to invade the southern state in later years. In 1283, the Mongols under Prince Thoat Hoan, invaded Vietnam but was badly beaten by marshal TRAN HUNG DAO. The famous Conference of Dien Hong was held in 1284 and the whole population was firmly united in its willingness to counterattack the Mongol invading forces. The Vietnamese were victorious at the battles of Ham Tu, Chuong Duong, Tay Ket and Van Kiep, at the amazement of the whole world.

**1253**

An-Nam (Vietnam) became a feudal state under the Mongols.

**1371**

The Champa forces invaded the Red River delta, vandalized Hanoi, and recaptured some of their lost provinces. This event led to an economic crisis which resulted in the fall of the Tran dynasty.

**1406-1428**

With the pretext of restoring the Tran dynasty, the Ming emperor of China used malicious measures and sly policies to dominate the Vietnamese people. The Chinese proclaimed Dai-Viet (Vietnam) a province of China.

**1428-1527**
The Le dynasty was founded by Le Loi, a farmer, who headed a ten-year rebellion against the Chinese, employing guerrilla tactics and strategies, and finally defeated the Chinese in 1427. He then founded the Le dynasty which lasted 360 years.

**1527**
Mac Dang Dung founded the Mac dynasty (1527-1592).

**1538-1788**
The latter Le dynasty. Real power was in the hands of the Nguyen and Trinh lords.

**1592**
The Trinh family took power from the Mac rulers.

**1600**
Nguyen Hoang was sent to Thuan-Hoa (Hue) and Quang-Nam (Central Vietnam). He established the Nguyen family government, south of Hanoi, independent of the Trinh family in North Vietnam. Both families claimed to support the Le emperor as a pretext to justify the civil strife they were indulging in for nearly two hundred years.

**1627**
Alexander de Rhodes, a Catholic priest, headed the French Christian mission in North Vietnam. He introduced the use of the Roman alphabet to represent the Vietnamese language quite successfully and this paved the way for future French influences in Vietnam in later years.

**1630**
Persecution of Christianity in North Vietnam. The first Vietnamese Catholic martyrs.

1635

The Dutch merchants opened trading posts in Hanoi, North Vietnam (circ. 1700).

1672

The English established a trading post in Pho-Hien (Central Vietnam).

1680

The French set up their trading posts in Pho-Hien.

1692

Baron Nguyen conquered the Champa and then the Khmer.

1776-1802

The Tay Son brothers rose up against the Nguyen warlords. Emperor Quang Trung defeated the Chinese at the Battle of Dong Da (1789).

1802-1945

The beginning of the Nguyen dynasty - the last dynasty of monarchial Vietnam. This dynasty was terminated when King Bao Dai abdicated in 1945.

1806

Freedom of religion was granted to Catholic missionaries.

1825

Christianity was again banned in Vietnam.

1832-1838

Vietnamese Christians were executed by the thousands.

**1861**

French forces captured Saigon (while the Civil War erupted in the U.S.A.).

**1862**

Emperor Tu Duc ceded three provinces of Cochinchina (South Vietnam) to the French, granting them broad religious, economic, and political concessions.

**1867-1945**

Cochinchina (South Vietnam) became a French colony.

**1873**

Hanoi was attacked by French expeditionary forces. Francis Garnier, a French officer, was killed by Vietnamese defenders.

**1874**

Central and North Vietnam were placed under the French Protectorate System.

**1882**

The second invasion of Hanoi by the French colonialist units. The Red River was forced to open to French trade with the southern provinces of China.

**1885-1895**

Several Vietnamese patriots revolted against French domination in Cochinchina.

**1887**

France created the Indochinese Union composed of Cochinchina (South Vietnam), An-Nam (Central Vietnam), Tonkin (North Vietnam), Cambodia and Laos.

**1914**

World War I broke out in Europe. Thousands of Vietnamese troops were recruited to serve in labor battalions in France.

**1915**

Opening of the Suez canal.

**1917**

Governor General Albert Sarraut signed the Code for Public Instruction. The French were deeply involved in their war against Germany.

**1918**

End of World War I. Flare up of the communist revolution in Russia. The French did not slacken their colonialist grip on Vietnam.

**1920**

Ho Chi Minh joined the newly formed French Communist Party, while numerous other nationalists formed revolutionary parties to resist against the French.

**1930**

Nguyen Thai Hoc's uprising against the French. He was arrested and sentenced to death. Ho and comrades formed the Indochinese Communist Party in Hong Kong.

**1931-1934**

The economic depression reached the shore of Vietnam. The revolutionary movements led by nationalist Vietnamese against the French were more active than ever.

**1932**

Japan invaded China.

1939

The French secretly helped the Indochinese Communist Party to organize a war zone to resist against the Japanese. (World War II flared up as German troops invaded Poland).

1941

The Japanese destroyed the U.S. naval force at Pearl Harbor on December 7th in a sneak attack.

1942-1945

Five consecutive governments exercised control over Vietnam.

1945

Saigon was seized by the French expeditionary corps. The Japanese transferred power in Indochina to the Vietnamese people. Throughout that period, some two million Vietnamese died of famine in North Vietnam.

1946

The Indochinese War broke out with the Vietnamese attack on the French in Hanoi. The war lasted for eight years (1946-1954) and ended with the Geneva agreement. The French had to leave Vietnam for good (1954).

1947

The Truman Doctrine was adopted. The U.S.A. tacitly agreed to let the French re-impose colonialism on their former possessions.

1949

Red China recognized the Ho Chi Minh government. President Truman approved 10 million dollars for the French forces in Indochina. (North Korea invaded South Korea).

1954
The Geneva agreement decided upon using the 17th parallel to partition Vietnam into two separate political entities: North Vietnam (under communist rule) and South Vietnam (under nationalist rule).

1945-1975
Political struggles and civil wars. The war reached its climax in 1965 when the United States sent in American troops to help South Vietnam. (See chapter on "One Perspective on the Vietnam War"). The Great Exodus started with nearly 150,000 Vietnamese fleeing from South Vietnam.

Senator Everett M. Dirksen, in March 1968, in his foreword to Rev. John J. O'Connor's book, "A Chaplain Looks at Vietnam," published by the World Publishing Company (Cleveland, Ohio), wrote: "The moral implications of the conflict in Vietnam and the United States' involvement there have not, to my knowledge, been presented clearly to the American people - until now (1968). Nor are they likely to be presented at any future time in such penetrating depth as within these pages. Chaplain O'Connor's analysis of the strategic situation in Vietnam is thoughtful and thorough in all respects - historical, military, diplomatic and economic. From it he (O'Connor) draws conclusions of moral consequence and strength that are enlightening, heartening, and of enduring significance." [4]

Those few words about Rev. O'Connor's book introduce a theme on various topics that are discussed such as factors that led the U.S.A. in the involvement in a country so distant from its shore. The candidate would like to recommend its reading to those American friends who want to know more about the conflict in that area of the world.

[4]*Everett M. Dirksen, Foreword to "A Chaplain Looks at Vietnam," by Rev. John J. O'Connor, The World Publishing Co., Cleveland, Ohio, 1968, p. ix.*

Additionally from Sen. Dirksen's foreword: "No mature American can deny that the best interests of the United States must ever and unfailingly be our first interest. But the best interests of this beloved country of ours must ever have their roots and base in moral strength as well as in material resources." [5]

The time for disagreement with and dissent from involvement in Vietnam is now over and it belongs to the history over one decade after the military upset. "The period of quarrelsome and dangerous assertions of those seeking personal publicity, power, and privilege" [6] is also over. The American public today is increasingly aware of the true meaning of involvement in foreign affairs and conflicts regarding communist expansion and subversion.

The dedication and sacrifice of American servicemen as well as those of Vietnamese nationalist combatants in the Vietnam War truly deserve our respect and admiration. [7] The presence of over 600,000 Vietnamese newcomers in this land of freedom and justice will remain an everlasting reminder that Americans and Vietnamese did not shed their blood in vain. They died so that others may live. Their memories are engraved in our hearts - the hearts of freedom-loving Americans and Vietnamese for ages to come.

The Vietnamese people even with their many years of upheavals and recently the Vietnam War always maintain characteristics of their cultural existence - that is their solidarity and unity - reaffirmed in these words by Senator Dirksen: "As without vision a people perish, so without moral concern and strength they cannot hope either to survive or to prevail. Firm and secure in our historic conviction that right does make might, we can be confident indeed that in this crisis, as in all others, we shall do both."

---

[5]*Ibid., p. ix.*
[6]*Ibid.*
[7]*Please read John K. Leba, "One Perspective of the Vietnam War," p. 37.*
[8]*Ibid., p. 5.*

## COURAGE AND MORALE

Historically, it has been shown that the Vietnamese people have great love for their country - evident by their expressed courage and strong resistance against invaders into their territory. Furthermore, the Vietnamese have great solidarity and unity of spirit in their continual struggles against invaders. Evidence of such spirit is that they maintained their traditions and customs amidst wars and upheavals and supported one another throughout these hardships.

According to a French historian, Aurousseau, in one of his studies on the origin and civilization of the Lac Viet (ancient name of Vietnam), he complimented the Vietnamese virtues by these words: "Thanks to those characteristics they could manage to unify the country from North to South. They had a system of governing with great homogeneity from one end of the nation to the other." [1] Vietnam was a unified country having one language with slight differences only in minor dialects. It was unified more so than in any area in China.

For instance, in China, in the province of Kwang-Tung there are so many vastly different dialects that each could be considered as a separate language. Not so in Vietnam where all the people can understand one another, immaterial if you are from North Vietnam or South Vietnam.

A French administrator, Pierre Pasquier, also had words of praise for the Vietnamese people in his book entitled Annam of the Old: "It would be to no avail if we were to use violence and military atrocities to deal with the Vietnamese people. Military threat will never win their friendship, for the Vietnamese people are courageous and do not fear death.

---

[1] *"Lac-Viet" by Aurousseau.*

They would not allow themselves to be subordinated by foreign invaders. They would be rebellious and would revolt continuously in spite of disastrous and violent measures used by the conquerors."[2]

Additionally, love of their land is presented in the historical work "Hoai Nam Tu" which has the following words for the Vietnamese people: "The Emperor Chin wanted very much to take the treasures from the southern regions, which included ivory tusks, rhinoceros tusks, precious stones and other valuable items. He sent a great general at the head of an army of 50,000 soldiers to invade the southern neighbors. It took three years for this army to invade the territory in the South (i.e. Vietnam)."[3]

The Vietnamese had to flee into jungles and set up their resistance forces against the troops sent by the Emperor Chin. The tribesmen elected strong leaders in their struggle against the Northern invaders. Subsequently, the Chinese were badly defeated; General Do Thu of the Chinese army was killed in one of the great battles along with tens of thousands of Chinese troops.

In spite of great efforts, the Chinese did not manage to subjugate the tribesmen in the South (Vietnam), who were great defenders of their land and heritage. The inhabitants cherished their villages to the extent of considering them as sacred sanctuaries. Their patriotism was also displayed by their deep feelings toward their country and their relentless defensive efforts.

Their country comprised of villages (or hamlets) in which they lived. At times Vietnamese families of five generations would live together under the same roof. This was customary

[2]*"Annam of the Old," Pierre Pasquier.*
[3]*"Hoai Nam Tu" (vol. 8 "Nhan Gian Huan")*

thousands of years ago and still is a prevailing custom today.

Also common was a system of labor exchange among families. For example, in building homes or reaping crops, no one family was without assistance from another in time of need. This practice of labor exchange fostered solidarity among the Vietnamese people even to this present date.

## CULTURAL INFLUENCES

The reader can imagine that due to the long periods under Chinese domination, sometimes even over a thousand years with some heroic uprisings in-between, the Vietnamese were most influenced by the Chinese four-class system in their societal and cultural structures.

Since businessmen were expressly categorized in the lowest social class in Vietnam until the end of the French rule (1945), the potential businessmen in the land had to alter cultural beliefs in addition to dealing with such problems as the lack of: capital, formal education, specialized training and business experience.

Throughout the long Chinese domination there were other influences besides the class system that the Chinese introduced to Vietnam, such as the various philosophical ideas and religious doctrines among which were Confucianism, Taoism, Buddhism and various other ideologies.

Confucianism was the chosen state cult (2nd century B.C.) and dominated the government, society, education and literature in Vietnam until recently. The era of Confucius was of philosophical debates and vigorous literary writings over such beliefs as:

*A greedy man dies of money-making,*
*a heroic knight dies for fame,*
*a successful man dies of striving after power,*
*and·the common people avoid death.*[1]

Here it seems only the "common" people would survive, while those who were over-ambitious to attain power and wealth and other earthly achievements would eventually be doomed due to their professional prowess and ambition. According to such philosophy, we see no encouragement whatsoever for the merchant to strive for great wealths. Thus, the candidate does not doubt that the Vietnamese newcomers, who are in business, would be doomed if they were to carry these beliefs into the running of their business.

Confucius said, "People who do not believe in the same things cannot do business with one another," [2] by which he means all that an individual could do would be just to follow his (the individual's) own convictions. Confucius said of himself: "I would even be willing to be a carriage driver if I knew that by so doing I could get rich by my own efforts. Since I cannot be sure, I will do what I like to do." [3]

In the beginning of this statement Confucius said that only people who think alike or those that are of similar thoughts should do business with one another. If a person followed this teaching in business he would automatically put a limit on his business growth potential. And if one followed only by his own convictions in business without any external viewpoints to challenge his thoughts or ideas, his failure rate would be extremely high due to his restricted communication with the outside world. In fact, his product or service is the direct result of communicating with the outside world. As today, we know marketing research is done so that the seller (businessman)

[1]*Molly Joel Coye and Jon Livingston, ed., "China: Yesterday and Today,"* *Bantam Books, Des Plaines, Ill. 60016, 1975, p. 61.*
[2]*Ibid., p. 40.*
[3]*Ibid., p. 40.*

produces the required product or service to meet the needs of the buyer (consumer). Without such necessary information the businessman is merely accepting some guesswork, which is absolutely contradictory to modern business practices.

The other part of the quoted statement defines the chance of accumulating wealth due to an obsession of probable failures, which is one of the biggest stumbling blocks of any businessman's success. Furthermore, one should not be consented with such passive attitude in order to compete in a capitalistic society such as the one prevailing in the U.S.A. where financial success or wealth accumulation is one of the greatest rewards of doing business. "Nothing ventured, nothing gained," so runs the maxim, accepted by all entrepreneurs.

Confucius also preached the Golden Rules in their negative form. He would tell his disciples: "Do not do unto others what you wouldn't want them to do unto you." or he would inform his follows: "Avoid doing wrong to others for you would not want this done unto you." Consequently, if an individual were to follow this concept, he would avoid doing wrong to others in the belief that others would do likewise. By following that teaching textually, the individual might not be guarded against malicious and felonious elements such as loan sharks and swindlers, who would really take advantage of their credulous clients - the borrowers and victims.

Next to Confucianism, the other very important stream of Chinese thoughts is Taoism (pronounced "daoism"). The Taoist belief is one of escaping from desires: "The man full in Tao (Taoism) does not get it into his mind to interfere with other men, because he will be content with himself and his place in nature. He is simple and without desires." [4]

---

[4]*Ibid.*, p. 48.

Taoist followers believed all things had equal claim to acceptance, and that one thing is not valued over another; besides, "any effort that is not spontaneous is affectation and therefore does not come from Tao."

The Taoists, through "sitting and forgetting" and "facts of the mind", experienced trance - like ecstasies in which they achieved the state of the "true man" and directly apprehend the oneness of the universe. Such practices may have been influenced by Indian yoga, for the Taoists, like the Indians, emphasized breathing exercises... [5]

Following this ideology one could not "desire" to be a businessman for it would naturally lead him to an environment where he believes that there are companies, products, services valued higher than others. If he followed that ideology he might feel reluctant in initiating market strategies so as to compete and gain a higher valued product in his line of business and, perhaps then, would fall along the wayside into bankruptcy.

Normal business activity and business planning, which could not be left to spontaneity, would not come from Taoism and therefore would go against the individual's convictions and cause conflict. This conflict would be a hindrance to the individual in business.

Another source of religious influences for the Vietnamese was the teaching preached by Buddha. Buddhism advocates these Four Noble Truths: [6]

1.- Man is destined for sufferance;
2.- The causes of sufferance originate from excessive desire;
3.- The cure for excessive desire is non-attachment to all

[5]*Ibid., p. 49*
[6]*"A Collection of Papers in Vietnamese Culture," Indochinese Culture Center, Houston, Texas, 1981, p. 22.*

things;

4.- The performance of non-attachment is the eightfold path: right conduct, right effort, right intention, right livelihood, right meditation, right mindfulness, right 'speech, and right view.

This too is contradictory to the ultimate goals of an ambitious businessman. The "modern" businessman in this competitive world must exert his best to increase sales that would in turn generate profit and wealth, which is his personal fortune and rewards.

Apart from the popular religious and philosophical practices which used to prevail in Vietnam, quite a number of Vietnamese believed in spiritism, pseudo-sciences, fortune-telling and superstitions. Many relied on these practices for predictions in their life when making important decisions. One can imagine how risky and unscientific this would be if business decisions were made on such bases alone.

In summary, the philosophy of life and religious beliefs among a great number of Vietnamese people became, in some respects, a form of barrier to their natural efforts as they transferred their residence from Vietnam to the United States. They had the burden of dealing with old deep-rooted systems and values. Therefore they would have to change their ways of thinking to parallel those in their new homeland. If they would not, their businesses would soon turn into failures because of the system conflicts within themselves. The Vietnamese newcomers, under influences of the Chinese four-class system, were mostly brought up with ideas that businessmen were "crooked" in one way or another in their business dealings because they made profits. [7] But here in the U.S.A., for those who choose to be in business, it is a very acceptable way of

---

[7]*"China: Yesterday and Today," The Four Classes by Dun Li, p. 56.*

making an honest living. Should these "businessmen want to make money even just to provide for their families, they had to alter their beliefs and attitudes towards the business world. Without those psychological changes the conflict would preclude the necessary motivation to make their businesses financial successes.

Vietnam was also influenced by the French social and economic policies from the period 1865 to 1945. The domination of that country by French colonialism had affected the Vietnamese culture in numerous ways. The French had maintained the then existing four-class system introduced and imposed by the Chinese. However, in addition to the class system, the French made education more difficult to attain and restricted it to foster slave mentality among the Vietnamese people and to serve the French colonial economic exploitation. The education available was usually contingent upon the political situation of the time.

During the period of French rule, interpreters and low ranking bureaucrats were needed for immediate communication with the conquered people. In this situation, it is understandable that the first school established by the French was aimed at training interpreters and translators. [8]

Years later the French authorities felt they no longer needed the interpreters, preferring direct contact and communication with the Vietnamese people. For this purpose they encouraged the French officers to learn the Vietnamese language, at the same time they began a program of teaching the Vietnamese to speak and write French. At that stage, all secondary education was instructed in the French language rather than in the native Vietnamese language.

---

[8]*"Vietnamese Culture", p. 85-106.*

The educational system was limited to only certain sections of the people, for only very restricted numbers of schools were available. "Modern" French education was offered only to those few who could successfully pass the very difficult examination papers required for each level of study.[9]

In the eighty years of domination the French managed in creating a society consisting of but a handful of educated elites with the majority or mass of common people working in low-ranking public clerical jobs, employed to implement and consolidate the colonial administrative machinery. In general, during the period (1865-1945), the Vietnamese were extremely hampered in term of education and general knowledge due to the harsh French colonialist policy. [10]

## INFLUENCES OF THE SOCIAL STRUCTURE

For the Vietnamese, there are cultural and social aspects and considerations that led to difficulty not only in their adjustment of working out ways and means to resettle in the United States, but additionally so for those who started their own business in the U.S.

Considering Vietnam's geographic features we can better understand the cultural and social influences it acquired from neighboring countries. Vietnam is situated on a peninsula called Indo-China with India to the west and China to the north. Vietnam was conquered by China several times - the longest period was over 1000 years.

Because of this long foreign domination, Vietnam's class stratification is quite similar to China's. In the meantime, her neighbors: Cambodia and Laos were much influenced by Indian culture, still evident mainly in their songs, dances and

[9]*"Vietnamese Culture"*, p. 85-106.
[10]*Ibid.*

scripts.

The caste system or class stratification in China - subsequently in Vietnam - is primarily a social stratification. Unlike in the United States, it is not classified according to wealth. In the U.S. society, the individuals are generally categorized into the lower, middle, upper middle, and high classes, measured according to the amount of wealth. Individual background is not of very great importance. In the U.S., if. an individual has a poor academic or cultural background but has great wealth he is considered in the top-most class. If no wealth is found in a highly educated man he is rather often classified as belonging to the lower middle class standing.

To the contrary, in China and Vietnam, the classification or stratification is as follows:

Customarily the Chinese spoke of their society as composed of four classes: the scholars, the farmers, the artisans, and the merchants. The scholars were given the highest status because they performed what the Chinese regarded as the most important function: the transmission of an ancient heritage and the personification of Chinese virtues. The farmers' standing was second only to the scholars because they were the primary producers, feeding and clothing the nation. The artisans processed what the farmers had produced, and their function was not regarded as so essential as that of the farmers. At the bottom of the social scale were the merchants whom the Chinese regarded as outright exploiters, making profits from what others had produced or processed and contributing nothing themselves. Two other classes were often added to the four described above. One was the soldiers, whose expected role of burning and killing was very distasteful to the Chinese. In as much as they took away the most valuable things from society, their standing in society was inferior to that of the merchants. Their image in the eyes of the public was not improved during modern times when the idle and adventurous swarmed to their ranks as mercenaries. The other class was the socalled "mean people" (chien-min), consisting of domestic slaves, prostitutes and entertainers. [1]

So the merchants classification did not yield a favorable image to the Vietnamese population. In fact "entrepreneurs" were considered to be crooked elements or even "thieves" because they made money off of other people's labor. This low stratification was brought about by the high-ranking officials (mandarins) who always considered themselves the cream of the social system. These mandarins, a highly educated group from old aristocratic families, based their power on scholarly achievements and extracted wealth from the farmlands through the collaboration of wealthy landlords. The mandarins were clairvoyant enough to predict that an increasing number of merchants were getting more and more wealthy. As the merchants started to acquire more riches, the administrators or mandarins became fearful that the former could gain power. They (the mandarins) therefore discouraged the profession with the class system. [2]

So if being an intellectual or administrator was considered to be the most prestigious in society, parents naturally encouraged their children to attain the highest academic degrees. On the other hand the merchants' way of life was expressly classified as the lowest and degraded profession and consequently not encouraged. Who could afford to educate their children to the degree required of a mandarin or officer? [3] Only the very wealthy. The great wealth usually was with the

---

[1]*"China: Yesterday and Today,"* The Four Classes by Dun Li, p. 56.
[2]*Ibid. et passim.*
[3]*Ibid.*

"big" farmers (large land-owners), so there was a link (of wealth and power) between the two classes: the administrators and the wealthy landlords.

Even if one wanted to stray from the normal professions to aspire to become a merchant, there was no education or training available to them. The schools were geared towards educating administrators, medical professions or scholars. Any skilled training in trades for ceramics, silverwares, fabric-weaving, rug-making, etc. was for the artisans. Moreover, since Vietnam was under the French domination for nearly 80 years (1865-1945), many "high-class" Vietnamese were educated in French as their first foreign language rather than English; this created a language barrier for the Vietnamese personally and in their business upon coming to the new land.

Furthermore the Vietnamese did not have the luxury of learning from experience and through apprenticeship, or having mentors because of the relatively few merchants in the Vietnamese society.

The class systems then adapted from the Chinese conquerors subsequently became barriers to the Vietnamese people in recent years as they set up business in their new homeland — the U.S.A.

In the first group of Indo-Chinese coming to the U.S. there were 150,000 people comprising of approximately 130,000 Vietnamese, 12,000 Cambodians and 8,000 Laotians, who were methodically spread throughout the states [4] so that no single state would feel any social and economic impact upon itself.

Most Vietnamese left their country in a hurry or rather

[4]*See Tables 2 and 3, pp. 65-66*

running for their lives before the onslaught by communist forces. Very few were fortunate enough to bring along their fortunes. Practically all had to leave their possessions behind with the exception of some fishermen who were able to bring their belongings including some hoarded gold in their fishing boats to the high seas, where they were picked up by U.S. naval ships and transported to safety on U.S. controlled bases such as Subic Bay, Guam, and Okinawa. Other than this small fortunate group, most others came empty-handed.

Writers, teachers, physicians and even high-ranking military officers, during the first months in the new land, took work as laborers to survive. Many worked as dishwashers at restaurants, laborers on construction sites, and in other menial jobs. But they were hardworking and courageous newcomers earning their living honestly.

The fishermen with their belongings and skills had come to shore and immediately started working and soon built up their new wealth. Additionally the medical professionals were exceptionally fortunate because Vietnamese newcomers needed Vietnamese-speaking physicians. Moreover most medical fees were covered through the U.S. Medicaid and Medicare programs which contributed considerably to the lucrativeness of the medical professions.

Other Vietnamese who by importing merchandise from Thailand, Hong Kong and Taiwan could cater specifically to their own people, providing the latter with food-stuffs and various products. Some could even produce and farm vegetables of familiarity which the expatriates preferred over other U.S. vegetables.

One phenomenon is entertainers (singers, dancers, etc.) who began to respond to the new overseas market were quite successful financially. In Vietnam, only a few entertainers could earn their living as easily as they do in the States.

So in many instances, marketing these products and services was not only profitable but booming, because of the immediate demand of the newcomers.

The artisans had a relatively easy adjustment to new life if they could find jobs usually in factories, working as technicians and assemblers. The people whose trades and professions were readily adaptable in the U.S. and those who came with cash on hand had made an easy adjustment; however, the majority found adjustment long and difficult.

Those who had professions or trades what were not easily transferrable to their newly-adopted homeland were the scholars (including poets, writers, teachers, lawyers, journalists, etc.), mandarins, administrators, officials and farmers.

The scholars had difficulty mainly because of the language barrier and the marketability of their expertise.

Farmers coming to the new land were not only unfamiliar with the new technical advances in agriculture but also unable to buy the land and machinery necessary to turn out products needed to compete with local U.S. farmers.

The mandarins and officials had extreme difficulty in adapting because they could no longer serve as public servants here in the United States even after years of resettlement in this country. Because the administrators, scholars, and wealthy farmers belong to the social classes that used to be highly respected in the former Republic of Vietnam, it was exceptionally hard for them to adjust to U.S. ways not only economically or financially but also in social and class standing.

These Vietnamese who had difficulty in adjusting had to learn new trades and professions. Many learned new skills in technology, photography, architecture, real estate, insurance, bookkeeping, and so forth.

Thus an evolution was taking place among the Vietnamese newcomers in the last ten years regarding social class and standing among themselves calling for changes and adjustments while they settle down in this country.

The Vietnamese newcomers, after a decade of settlement in their new homeland, could be reclassified as follows:

1) The new wealthy class: The well organized fishermen, a number of fast money-making medical professionals, former corrupt high-ranking officials who pilfered public funds, dishonest merchants who made great fortunes dealing with communist trading agencies;
2) Successful businessmen and medium fishermen;
3) Liberal professionals, engineers, architects, entertainers, publishers;
4) Technicians, factory workers, skilled laborers, etc.

A later chapter will discuss the various trades and businesses being carried out by the Vietnamese newcomers in this country during the recent decade.

# Chapter 2
# BACKGROUND OF THE STUDY

- One Perspective on the Vietnam War.

- The Boat People - A Phenomenon.

- New Life of the Overseas Vietnamese

- The First Decade in the U.S.A.

Distribution of Asian peoples and cultures.

# ONE PERSPECTIVE ON THE VIETNAM WAR

## (1945-1975)

The author admits that a number of viewpoints presented in this paper are subjective in character. Nevertheless, he still feels that they represent at least one particular perspective on the Vietnam War and he gladly welcomes other ideas and opinions as long as they help bring to light this very important topic before the public sentiment regarding the Vietnamese as well as Americans. The writer urges the reader to spare the time in contributing his objective viewpoints on this subject. Ten years have passed, yet the problems of the Vietnam War are still open for discussion and debate. Journalists, historians and commentators have offered their perspectives, some impartial while others are blatantly biased.

## TEN YEARS HAVE PASSED

Over 125,000 Vietnamese people, in the initial stage of the exodus, had to flee from their native land in order to avoid living under the communist regime, whose atrocities they knew fully well. This year has marked the tenth aniversary they have been away from their Fatherland.

In the early days of May, 1975, antiwar waves in the U.S.A. were still very strong. They seemed to make their final efforts in driving those miserable refugees back to the ocean. But thanks to a clever and well-planned program for resettlement implemented by the Ford Administration, those refugees were admitted orderly and peacefully into this country. The program was successful thanks to proper selection of locations away from metropolitan areas in order to receive such great numbers of refugees. In the course of only six months, almost

150,000 Indochinese newcomers, including 12,000 Cambodians and 8,000 Laotians, have been deployed all over the 50 states, thus reducing all emotional reactions from the narrow-minded antiwar and racist elements.

The "Vietnamese Syndrome" was of course prevailing in 1975 and even in 1976. By the end of 1977, Jimmy Carter won the election, but through his numerous and continuous setbacks in matters of politics, diplomacy, strategy and economics, the American people gradually began to wake up from illusions, by showing signs to be less affected by that defeatist syndrome.

When we read in the press or watch the TV, if we hear American politicians and well-known commentators frequently say: *"We don't want another Vietnam,"* we have to say to ourselves: "To them, Vietnam implies the following meanings: a political turmoil, a military defeat, a bacterium to be shunned... Vietnam is a dangerous epidemic to be scared of."

It would have been untimely to analyze the "Vietnam Syndrome" back in 1975-76, though the writer wished he could have done so then, but after reflection, he thought it might be wiser to shelve the analysis. Today the situation is turning toward a quite different trend, and more American people are having outspoken attitudes vis-à-vis the "Vietnam War."

## SIX AMERICAN PRESIDENTS

When the words: *"We don't want another Vietnam"* are said by American intellectuals, this humble writer only wishes to retort: *"What's wrong with Vietnam?"*

If they advocate that the Vietnam issue has been wrong all along, could it be possible that six American presidents from Truman (1945-1954), Eisenhower (1954-1962), Kennedy (1962-1963), Johnson (1963-1968), Nixon (1968-1974), to Ford (1974-1976), with hundreds of highly intellectual secretaries and aides serving in their administrations, be all wrong?

If they were not entirely wrong, they must have been *partially right*. Why haven't there been any people who have ever asked: *"What's right with Vietnam ?"* or *"Isn't there anything right with Vietnam?"*

## THE UNITED STATES AND VIETNAM

Let's turn back a few pages of history concerning Vietnam. The reader should remember that it was not in 1963 that the U.S., under the leadership of President Kennedy, began to be directly involved in Vietnam, but in fact, it started as far back as 1941. The United States with bases in Chung-King (Sze-Chuan, China) was scrupulously following the situation in Vietnam. Every single movement of the Japanese Imperial Forces on the Indochinese peninsula was carefully and minutiously scrutinized by American intelligence. Only one year after Pearl Habor (1941), the entire territory of Indochina, especialy North Vietnam, was under terrifying air raids by American bombers based in Chung-King, Kunming, Nanning and Mongtse, or from carriers plying along the Gulf of Tonkin and the South China Sea.

Immediately after the end of World War II (1945), obsessed by the fact that Indochina might be swallowed up by communist regimes, the United States hurriedly agreed to let the French imperialists reestablish colonialism over the peoples of Vietnam, Cambodia and Laos (1946). The Franco-Vietnam War officially broke out on December 19, 1946, marking a new era in colonialist warfare.

However, world situation was unexpectedly changing at a new precipitous momentum. The Koumintang regime in China was rapidly falling apart before the overwhelming onslaught of the Red Army, under the leadership of Mao Tse-Tung. Because of poverty and miseries, the Chinese people leaned towards the communist leadership like ripened rice-stalks under whirlwinds. By 1948, most of the important industrial cities in North China fell into the hands of Red Chinese. The stronghold of Tsi-an — which supplied most of the ammunition to the Nationalist forces — also fell. On the other hand, the U.S. cut off all military reinforcements from the regime of Generalissimo Chiang Kai Shek. The inevitable consequence was that by late September, 1949, the entire mainland of China was conquered by the communists.

With the new situation in view, as early as 1950 the French were aware of the fact that they could not win, if not to say that they would lose, the war in face of the communist Sino-Vietnamese alliance. However, under the influence of the Domino Theory (communism might spread its sway over South East Asia) the U.S. exerted pressure on the French so that the latter would carry on the war. All war expenses incurred by the French Expeditionary Forces would be footed by the American Government. This stage of the war was understood as the Proxy War (1951). The French defeat at Dienbienphu,[1] 1954, announced the end of the Franco-Viet War. The result of the war was the partition of Vietnam along the 17th parallel.

---

[1] *In reality, a great number of Red Chinese units also participated in this great battle in addition to the Vietnamese communist units involved.*

## THE ROLE OF COMMUNIST CHINA

Immediately after having conquered the entire territory on mainland China (1949-50), the Chinese Communists thought they could expand their domain further more, and at the same time they would be able to break the containment policy advocated by the U.S. They plotted with North Korea to open a new war theater. This was the Korean War which broke out in 1951 aiming at two main targets: conquering South Korea and at the same time diverting the U.S. from Vietnam. But facing extremely strong reaction of most UNO member-nations and especially that of the U.S.A., the North Korean ambitions could not be materialized. The North Korean communist regime of Kim Il Sung narrowly escaped being shattered, if Big Brother China had not deployed over one million troops to help him out.

The Korean War ended in 1953. In spite of the shorter duration of the war, casualties in human lives and material destructions by both sides were more enormous than those involved in the Franco-Vietnamese War (1945-1954). We can figure out how the Korean War was closely related to the Franco-Vietnamese War. It obviously manifested the expansionism policy advocated at that time by the Chinese Communists. We should also be aware of the fact that Mao Tse-Tung was the only important communist leader that had never been directly trained by Moscow. His philosophy and doctrine were following a very special and different course. His viewpoints vis-à-vis international issues were relatively short-sighted and restrained. Because of this particularity, Mao and Chu Teh were at times underestimating the forces and fighting morale of the Allied forces (the Democratic Bloc). In the interim, more pragmatic party members such as Chu En Lai, Teng Shiao Ping, Yeh Chien Ying, Hwang Hua... were having progressive thoughts, but dared not offer their suggestions for fear of the henchmen of Chiang Ching (Mao's wife) who at that time was wielding too much power.

With the French defeat in Vietnam, the Americans inevitably had to come in to take over the former's place. As of this stage began the role of Ngo Dinh Diem who was invited by the Americans to return to Vietnam (1954). Uninterruptedly from 1954, the U.S. put out its greatest efforts in introducing its military advisory teams into South Vietnam (eventually called the Republic of Vietnam) in order to modernize the latter's military machinery. A record change was imposed on the overall modernization of the armed forces of the Republic of Vietnam. From small combat units attached to the French Expeditionary Forces, the ROV military units soon turned into the most crack combat units in the world.

Ironically enough, as the Vietnamese Nationalist armed forces showed proofs of maturity, the nepotistic regime, advocated by the Ngo family, also prevailed with the same momentum. The writer does not wish to include his criticism on the shortcomings of that family-rule regime which culminated at its climax during the years 1959 to 1963.

We should also recall that during the Eisenhower Administration, State Secretary John Foster Dulles (1953-1959) was a man who nurtured the greatest antagonism towards communism, and his brother Allen Dulles — the CIA chief — did bring some special influence on American foreign policy during that period. In order to counter the Domino Theory, they put into application the Policy of Containment to obstruct the Chinese Communists from territorial ambition. This tactics was to make use of all means to set up a gigantic barrier around China — thus isolating Red

China from the rest of the world.

We should not pass judgment that J. Foster Dulles was in the wrong. In fact, during the initial years of victory (1950-1960) the Chinese Communists did have the ambition of expanding their territory. In an interview in Saigon, Vietnam, between Ambassador Cabot Lodge and the JCI President, the ambassador invited his guests, among whom was the author, to view a mural map of "New China" recently printed in Peking (1964). On that new official map of the People's Republic of China, it was indicated that the "New China" would comprise Korea, Taiwan, the Philippines, East and West Malaysia, Singapore running through to Burma... all those countries would lie within China's proper!! This also means that Vietnam, Cambodia and Laos as well as Thailand should be encompassed in the "Greater China." [2] Naturally, how could such ambition be materialized? Surely there had to be some sort of accountable motif to curtail those ambitions. We believe that that "new" map is now scrapped in some Chinese museum, and that the Chinese people must accept a pragmatic policy (which will be discussed in a latter part of this subchapter).

**AFTERMATH OF THE GENEVA CONFERENCE**

The consequence of the Geneva Conference in 1954 was the partition of Vietnam. A very significant measure was advocated by the U.S.A., which was the establishment of the South East Asian Treaty Organization (SEATO) comprising nine nations all having interests in that region. Later, the Free World witnessed the participation in the War by military contingents from Australia, New Zealand, Indonesia, Thailand, the Philippines, and South Korea (with the exception of England and France). Today there is no longer

---

[2]*That was the dream of the former leaders of China. It is hoped that the incumbent rulers of that country will carry out a more pragmatic policy.*

any reason for SEATO to exist when the Republic of Vietnam fell into the hands of the Viet Communists at the end of April, 1975. In brief, the two blocs had been dealing hard blows at each other during those past few decades.

## HOW THE SOVIETS GRAB AT OPPORTUNITIES

The Watergate incident, which led to President Nixon's historical resignation, also brought about further success to anti-war activists. The latter preached that whatever assistance the Nationalist Vietnamese would have could only mean the prolongation of the War. When President Ford took over the reins of the Administration, a part of his job was the preparation of the death certificate - the Paris Peace Agreement - for the second Republic of Vietnam. Another of his jobs was the arrangements for the gigantic evacuation in the best order that could be thought of. We also witnessed how the Ford administration would like to shun the "Vietnam Syndrome." When assuming power, President Carter never deemed to touch on the Vietnam Affair, except that he might once in a while sign into laws a few bills of a more humanitarian nature so as to extend assistance to boat-people on the high seas and refugees scattered in camps all over South East Asia.

We must bear in mind that: wherever and whenever the communists see any weak points in the adversary's camp, they would exploit those points without hesitation. The American government, during that certain period, took the position of demagogy towards its people to the extent of completely doing away with the selective military service. On the other hand, several key figures of the CIA, FBI... were reprimanded, exposed, or indicted. How could national secrets be protected effectively under such circumstances? The god-sent opportunity for the communists to take advantage of had come.

We all know too well of the expansionist policy of the Soviets:

- Using political and diplomatic ruses in order to attain advantages is their top policy, such as in the cases of Yalta, Potsdam... The most profits could be reaped at the least expenses.

- Making use of propaganda to blast the adversary, which may lead to "cold wars" as in the blockade of West Berlin.

- Applying diplomatic appeasement which they termed "détente" (Vietnam, Helsinki...) if the cold wars proved unsuccessful. This political ploy is also defined as the Soviets' "midway policy" or "compromise."

- Complying to some concession if necessary, as we have recently witnessed what some Russian communist leaders were trying to maneuver at the various disarmament talks. When the U.S. negotiators talk tough, their Soviet counterparts will talk soft. This is because the Russian bear dare not bully a tough leader like Reagan.

- Plotting with their lackeys to foment troubles and, if necessary, overthrowing governments and grasping the reins of power as in Angola, Mozambique, Ethopia. And if needs be, the Soviets themselves would handle the "dirty" job as they have been doing in Afghanistan.

- Starting real hot wars of actual shooting and killing with lots of bloodshed as in Nicaragua, El Salvador... is considered their *least advantageous policy.*

Considering the long implanted and classical Soviet policies, we can trace out the strategem that the U.S. had been adopting in the course of the Vietnam war.

## DID THE U.S.A. COMMIT A "GAFFE"?

Did the U.S.A. really make a gaffe in the Vietnam War as so many people thought? In 1968-1970, the U.S. and the Republic of Vietnam managed to deal a rather decisive blow on the communist forces. Why didn't the U.S. policy-makers take advantage of the situation to end the war? After the Tet General Offensive (1968), the Viet Cong suffered a major defeat — many of their crack divisions were deployed to the various fronts for reinforcements. The furious air attacks inflicted by the U.S. in communist territories created great impacts on the morale of the people in North Vietnam. Many of those who recently came from North Vietnam made it known that if the air raids had lasted for some more time and if the U.S. had deployed about 5 divisions to effect a landing operation on North Vietnam as it did at Inchun in Korea, the outcome of the Vietnam War would have been quite different.

The author does not think the U.S. miscalculated and missed a good opportunity. As already mentioned in an earlier part of this paper, if a mistake had been made, it would have been made perhaps by one or two American presidents — but how could six presidents have made the same mistake? In the writer's opinion, the Vietnam War was a "Great Decoy". According to a Chinese book on warfare, the American tactics is comparable to that of "martial arrays in the west, actual attacks in the east." Let's discuss this further.

The years 1966-1968 were culminated by the Tet Offensive and the eye of the whole world was focusing on the Vietnam theater. Speaking in a broader sense, the War between the Democratic Bloc and the Communist Bloc was at that time concentrated on the Vietnam front. And this is the position of "martial arrays or saber-rattling in the west."

However, during that same period, what was happening elsewhere? A new era for American diplomacy and strategy had just started, and the U.S. wanted to carry out its new policy as tactfully and discreetly as possible. This is a very remarkable turning point.

## "SABER-RATTLING IN THE WEST; ATTACKS IN THE EAST"

After a tough trial of martial feats without winners or losers, and for a period of ferocious punishment on the Chinese and Vietnamese communists by the U.S. weaponry (in Korea and in Vietnam), the Chinese were fully aware of the might of their counterpart (the U.S.). They were then ready to accept the Ping Pong Diplomacy in 1968.

All the while, Kissinger was quietly negotiating with the Chinese Communists (since 1968) so that by the beginning of 1970, and at the astonishment of the whole world, Kissinger flew from Tashkent to pay a royal visit to Chairman Mao! Only one year after, President Nixon was found sitting at his famous dinner with Chu En Lai, and also in the presence of Mao and Chu Teh, toasting one another longevity and best of luck!" [3]

Simultaneously, the U.S. was secretly finding means and ways to overthrow President Sukarno of Indonesia. This is

---

[3] *Not long after that dinner, Mao, Chu Teh and Chu En Lai all three followed one another to visit Carl Marx - their mentor.*

48

also another significant point in the overall strategy. The readers are requested to look at the map of South East Asia and they will notice that Sumatra is separated from Malaysia by the very narrow Strait of Malacca. If that body of water were not infested with deadly sharks, humans could even swim from Sumatra to Malaysia.

The geographical features of these two nations are here raised in order to point out the close and important relationship between Indonesia and the entire Indochina Peninsula.

From 1954 to 1967, the policy advocated by Red China had always been the creation of a Sino-Indonesian Alliance, with which it could wield supremacy over South East Asia. Indonesia is a country with over 150 million people, ranking it as the 5th nation in population. It has an area of 600,000 square miles with abundant natural resources such as: petroleum, zinc, tin, iron ore, alumna, rubber, rice, sea products...

In face of a prospective Sino-Indonesian Alliance, Japan, Taiwan (Republic of China), the Philippines and quite naturally, Vietnam, Cambodia, Laos, Thailand and Malaysia would be forced to their knees. Japan is the most industrialized nation among its neighbors, but it is hopelessly poor in natural resources. Consequently, Japan's position is the most precarious. Without raw materials, especially petroleum, Japan would be like a stranded fish (completely powerless).

Regarding Mr. Sukarno, he wielded power handed over to him by the Dutch since 1949. He was a very ambitious man who loved honor and publicity. He was specially fond of young pretty girls, but at the same time he also liked to fondle with Marxism. His country is so rich in natural resources yet his people were among the most poverty-stricken. He liked to play the role of wall-sitting not much different from the attitude advocated by Sihanouk of Cambodia just to win the attention of the world. But when the U.S. interests had to suffer and when its strategic positions were in jeopardy, it (the U.S.) would have to work out plans to get rid of Sukarno in 1967. Thus, after 18 years in power, Sukarno was overthrown and the following year he left this world to return to Allah. The game of politics is so costly and dangerous!

## THE BALANCE OF POWER

Substituting Sukarno is President Suharto — a talented general, who is rather popular among his people. This new personality has a clear-cut political line to lean towards the Democratic Bloc.

The following opposing power struggle structure is to be scrutinized:

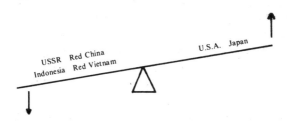

There wouldn't be any balance of power then! And the prospect of the Free Bloc would surely be gloomy and in peril! But thanks to the Vietnam War — the tactics of "saber-rattling in the west" — that eventually would lead to "actual offensive in the east" — meaning the drawing of China (over

1,000 million people) and Indonesia into the U.S. orbit. The U.S. has absolutely and undeniably succeeded in creating the current power structure in its favor in that area:

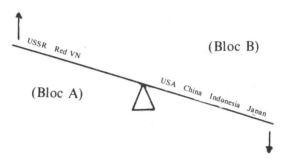

In Europe, the USSR is in a very disadvantageous situation. Today, it can only expect to exploit the turmoils in South West Asia, Africa and Latin America.

If we would just assume that the two opposing camps were of equal weight, we cannot, in practice, deny the fact that Bloc B actually is weightier than Bloc A. And this is not to mention the very problematic and thorny situations among the Warsaw Pact nations (erosions in the Warsaw bloc): most of the Eastern European nations are only waiting for the propitious moment to revolt against Big Brother. Up to this stage, we find that as our mathematical (or political) quiz is approaching nearer and nearer to its solution, we have an elaborate answer to the question: "Why did the U.S. not want a military victory in Vietnam?" That's easy to understand now!

## CHINA GATE

If the U.S. had been victorious in Vietnam with, say, 20 divisions deployed all over North Vietnam, it would have had immediate confrontation and provocation with communist China along the Sino-Vietnamese borders. So, why not make use of the Red Vietnamese constable to handle the job of guarding "China Gate"? It would certainly be more efficient and less expensive!

The U.S. knows quite well that the Han people (Chinese) and the Viet people have been antagonistic for thousands of years. The Vietnamese, though their nation is small in comparison with China, have proved to be the most stubborn towards their northern neighbors. After only three years, what the Americans were expecting began to materialize — and that was the bloody and destructive encounter between the Red Chinese and Red Vietnamese. That was the "first lesson" given to each other by the Chinese and Vietnamese. History will some day have this to say: "The first armed conflict between two communist nations was launched in earnest by the Red Chinese and the Red Vietnamese." In addition, the Red Vietnamese also deployed their armed forces to crush the Red Cambodians (Khmer Rouge). And that was another "historical event" highlighted by the Red Vietnamese in the "History of Mutual Annihilation of Communist Forces."

## IS THERE ANY MEANING IN THE VIETNAM WAR?

Having considered, in a general manner, the key events during the past three decades, we would like to bring up this question: "Should the American people think that their husbands, brothers and sons shed their blood in vain in the Vietnam War?" The writer deems it that those combatants did fight for the very survival of the United States as well as for the Free World. For, without the Vietnam War, how could there be the balance of power as described in an earlier part of this subchapter? Of late, there has been a feeling of dissatisfaction

, and frustration that American veterans, returning from Vietnam, did not receive any warm home-welcoming; on the contrary, there were even circumstances where they were shown the cold shoulder. The writer believes that those combatants indeed had fulfilled the obligations entrusted to them by their country. The brave fighting men of the Republic of Vietnam also manifested great feats of heroism worthy to be called first-rate troops second to none. But, again, they belonged to the fighting units that were doomed for defeat because of political reasons!

In Vietnam, the War was not aimed at military victories, but rather at the realization of a policy called the "strategy of martial arrays in the west in order to launch the actual offensive in the east." This strategy for creation of a new alliance in the world has steered the Nationalist Vietnamese to the sorrowful and heart-breaking conditions in Spring, 1975. In fact, when Henry Kissinger succeeded in building contacts with the Chinese communists in 1969-1970 the U.S. had started the implementation of its political plans for a new era. When Nixon made his official visit to Peking (1972), his plans for the Vietnamization of the war in Vietnam was also simultaneously under way. At the conclusion of the Paris Convention, punctuated by an agreement totally disadvantageous to the Nationalist Vietnamese (1973), the U.S. had already completed its orderly withdrawal from that war-torn country.[4]

The Paris Agreement can be considered as the death certificate for the Second Republic of Vietnam. Ironically enough, Le Duc Tho and Kissinger were awarded the Nobel Peace Prize! The Nationalist Vietnamese painfully watched that happen, but knowledgeable circles knew too well that that very agreement had the capability of bringing an end to the

---

[4]*In 1972, Nixon ordered full-scale air attacks over North Vietnam before ordering implementation of his Vietnamization plans. Maybe this was to have some final satisfaction (for his hatred of communism).*

Vietnam War and the extinction of Free Vietnam!

## LAMENTABLE ENDING

With the intention of weakening the incumbent administration of the Second Republic of Vietnam (during the two final years especially) the U.S. introduced or recommended a list of "kiddie ministers." Freshly graduated from American colleges, these greenhorns without the least experience were to participate in the various cabinets! Ironically, special attention was focused on the ministries which were the most prone to corruption. Anyhow, Thieu could boast that he had the youngest ministers in his administration in the entire world — for some of them were barely over 20-30 years old.

The readers may recall that those youthful ministers were holding great responsibilities for economic affairs, finance, labor, information... and directors-general holding the reins of offices of great importance such as: the bureau of taxes, customs... very lucrative positions indeed! This took place during the final years of the Thieu regime! The more widely corruption spread, the weaker Thieu's regime became. Despite the Vietnamese Nationalist combatants' outstanding performance on the battlefields, it was undeniable that their morale was much affected by the bad examples set by corrupt high-ranking officials.

What was worse was the fact that the U.S. began to cut short all forms of aid, especially military assistance at the very time when the ARVN[5] needed it most in order to counter the spearheads launched by the Vietnamese communists... at a time when flight sorties were restricted due to shortage of fuel, lubricants and bombs, at a time when artillery units were all

---

[5]ARVN: *Armed Forces of the Republic of Vietnam.*

running out of ammunition. How could the courageous combatants carry on the fights?!

On the other hand, anti-corruption movements were systematically organized in order to overthrow Thieu, the sooner the better... aiming at ending the Vietnam War and handing over the remaining territories in South Vietnam to the Vietnamese communists. This maneuver was not, in the least, aimed at making way for some other Nationalist Vietnamese to take over the reins of power or to revamp the cabinet. In brief, in the course of 1973-74, the U.S. was already making preparations for the events that were to happen in Spring, 1975. Ways and means as well as financial appropriations had been worked out to receive the thousands of Indochinese refugees who were to resettle on American soil...

The Vietnam War witnessed a tremendous sacrifice of the Nationalist Vietnamese. When the great interests of the Democratic Bloc were brought up for evaluation and appraisal, the Nationalist Vietnamese found themselves as only offerings to be sacrificed for the sake of the Great Cause — the Free World's Interests. The Vietnamese Nationalists are comparable to pawns in a chess game. When the time comes, in order to avoid a checkmate, the pawns will be sacrificed.

## A NEW ATTITUDE IS NEEDED

Now more than ever, the American public must adopt a new attitude, especially their attitude towards the veterans who fought courageously in Vietnam. In comparing the great sacrifices and perils encountered by those combatants, with ordeals experienced by the 52 hostages held in captivity by the Iranians, the latter would seem to have gone through minimal tests. And yet, the hostages were welcomed home with such pomp and fuss while the veterans seemed to have been neglected, or welcomed home with coolness and indifference. Where is fairness? Where is encouragement? We think it is about time now that the American people should not continue to be obsessed by the "Vietnam War".

The author hopes that his viewpoints in this brief study could contribute a modest part in the analysis of the "Vietnam Syndrome," which in the first place, should not have existed. If this complex is to be nurtured with fear and oversight, it will not be long before the United States becomes a power ranking second to the Soviet Union, encouraging the latter to continue to create events similar to those we already witnessed in Afghanistan, Mozambique, Nicaragua... The time may come when most of Africa would be swallowed up in the Red Deluge. The United States, the ultimate stronghold to offer effective defense to the Free and Democratic Bloc, might eventually be encircled on all fronts by the enemy. Would it be too late?

## BOAT PEOPLE — A PHENOMENON

There are some Americans, even today, who ask the Vietnamese newcomers: "Why did you choose the U.S. as your new home?" rather than asking more significantly: "How is it that you decided to leave your homeland?", "Was it a safe departure?", "How are you adjusting?" The Vietnamese did not want to leave the former Vietnam but had to in order to take refuge from communist atrocities. For the Vietnamese, leaving their Fatherland was emotionally difficult and life-threatening.

Vietnam is an agricultural land, and Vietnamese worked arduously with the land to produce their daily subsistence. The rich farmland was the product handed down by their ancestors. Attachment to the land through personal sentiment, and the influences of Confucianism made the decision of leaving their hand extremely difficult.

However, after the fall of Saigon into communists' hands on April 30, 1975, hundreds of thousands of Vietnamese, Cambodians and Laotians (collectively called Indochinese) fled for their freedom and human rights, leaving behind their land and properties, even their beloved parents, brothers, sisters and friends.

The refugees escaped communist Vietnam by way of the South China Sea on tiny frail motor-boats or wooden sampans without any kind of navigational instruments, adequate food supplies and water. Some were rescued on the high seas but the majority endured hardships from the treacherous weather conditions and atrocities of Thai (Thailand) pirates.

Those experiences on the high seas were tragic and perilous. As one survivor, Van, explained in an article written about his voyage: "I knew the chances of getting 140 people across the South China Sea on a 55 ft. riverboat were slim, but we had to leave".[1]

Van, having just been released from six years of hard labor in a prison camp met a man who was a member of a "secret organization" that arranged refugee sea-crossings in exchange for gold. Because he was chosen captain of the escape boat, Van did not have to pay. But he knew of payments up to U.S. $20,000 in gold to get aboard the riverboat, while for many they indeed paid with their lives.

Without proper navigational aids, boat people could get lost easily on the high seas. Food and water were gone after four days and their engine failed shortly thereafter. Burial at sea was continuous and one of the victims was Vinh's own pregnant wife.

Finally rescued, he said, "I love my country and I didn't want to leave, but we suffered too much." The former navy lieutenant junior grade began to sob.[2]

If the lack of food and water and dangerous weather conditions weren't enough adversities, the Vietnamese boat people were almost certain of being attacked by Thai pirates who would kill the men and rape the women and girls.

As an account, here is an excerpt from a 16-year-old girl, Nguyen Phuong Thuy, describing how she was kidnapped and put upon a Thai pirate boat: "I was locked up in a room. I

---

[1] "Thong Nhat Thoi Bao" (United Times), Houston, Texas, July 15, 1983, p. 12.
[2] "The San Diego Union," 4 August 1981, Sec. A, p. 7, cols 1-2.

tried to steal a look from the cracks. The pirates rammed their boat against our smaller boat which sank after the second hit. I saw my younger sister waving her hands and slowly swallowed up among the waves. It was a harrowing sight. I closed my eyes, refusing to look at the scene of the boat and people slowly drowning." [3]

She had what seemed an endless ordeal for four months... "I was raped in one boat after another. And by sheer luck, when I was taken onto the 15th boat, the skipper released me because it was their annual merit-making season (Sept. 25) drawing near in this region. He didn't want to commit a sin," she said.[4]

Another typical incident: N.C. Nguyen, a former military officer in Vietnam, who now lives in Houston, Texas, recalls his ordeal in April 1979. Nguyen and 20 other Vietnamese including three young women were fleeing to Malaysia in a small fishing boat. It was night, and they were well off the Vietnamese eastern coast when a Thai fishing boat approached. It carried nine bearded men with guns, knives and clubs.

"They jumped on board and made us all strip," recalled Nguyen.[1] The men found what little money the refugees had and threw the latter's clothes into the water." Then Nguyen said, "They began raping the women including one eighth-month pregnant. They carried out their barbarous acts right in front of us for hours," he said. "It was terrible, just terrible." [5]

These testimonials are but a few of the countless ordeals. For example, in 1981, of the boats that reached the shores of Thailand, 500 women and girls had been raped, 243 kidnapped and 571 men and women were cold-bloodedly murdered. [6]

[3]Pramasin Dilokpreechankum, "I Was Raped in 14 Boats" (extracted from "Cong Dong" (The Community) a local tabloid, published in Houston, Texas, November 1984.
[4]Ibid.
[5]Jo nathan Dahl, "Piracy Protection," Houston Chronicle.
[6]"Thong Nhat Thoi Bao" (United Times), Houston, Texas, December 1982, p. 28.

We wonder how such atrocities could escape the attention of the Thai government. Countries including Norway, West Germany, France, Holland and the U.S. have since launched repeated humanitarian appeals to the Thai government, but to little avail.

To these outcries Pracha Guna-Kasem of the Thai government said: "It is about time that the international community must try to solve this problem at its source by bringing the weight of world public opinion and conscience to bear on the Vietnamese Government to ease "exporting" their own population in such a callous, disorderly and extremely dangerous manner." [7]

So, who is assisting the Vietnamese in their departures from Vietnam?

Nguyen, the above mentioned refugee said of his people: "We want to do anything we can. Most of us still have a lot of family members back there." [8] About 600 Vietnamese in one fund-raiser contributed more than $25,000 for Operation Rescue headed by a retired Air Force colonel. The program is for the rescue of and assistance to refugees fleeing Vietnam, for locating the whereabouts of and negotiating release of women kidnapped by pirates; for promoting the return from Vietnam of Amerasian children; and for collecting information on the location of live Americans being held against their will in Southeast Asia and missing in action (M.I.A.) currently some 2,483. (At the time of this writing, Operation Rescue was hopelessly in dire financial situation and might have to terminate its activities altogether.)

There were company-owned (private industry) ships out at sea but they did not care to pick up refugees, because the legal

---

[7]*Pracha Guna-Kasem, "A Pool of Vessels for VN Refugees," The Nation Review, p. 16, col. 6.*

[8]*Jonathan Dahl, "Privacy Protection," Houston Chronicle, Houston, Texas*

work involved tied up the company boats. A few would assist in food and water.

Furthermore, the United Nations rescue committee is currently trying to locate the whereabouts of the kidnapped women and girls. Success is extremely slim. For example, out of the 483 that were kidnapped in the years 1981 and 1982, only 199 were found. [9]

A Vietnamese educator, commenting on the plight of the boat-people, said: "When a more or less famous sportman got lost on his sailing boat in a courageous attempt to cross the Atlantic in order to win a medal or a prize, the media would charter helicopters and governments would send squadrons of airplanes to look for him, and if by bad luck the would-be champion drowned, world public opinion would join in paying tribute to a modern hero! What about the hundreds, the thousands, the tens of thousands who drown and risk doing it every day of the week in the South China Sea? Do they not deserve a headline or an honorable mention?" [10]

In the face of great dangers and loss of lives among the refugees, the U.S. Government and the communist authorities in Vietnam did establish in 1979 a program called ODP (Orderly Departure Program). Thanks to this humanitarian program tens of thousands of people have been admitted into the U.S. through official channels rather than by hazardous and perilous means. However, most Vietnamese who have been processed through this program are sophisticates of a fallen elite. In some cases it would take only eight to nine months while others have been waiting since the program began. Refugees claim bribes must often be offered to communist officials to speed up paperwork. [11] This group of the ODP are "the jumbo jet" refugees. Vietnamese boat

---

[9]*"Voice of Free Vietnam," Houston, Texas, June 2, 1983.*

people still outnumber the jumbo jet refugees, but there are recent indications that more are opting to fight red tape, and pay bribes rather than expose themselves to pirates and stormy seas where the death toll is unofficially estimated in the hundreds of thousands.

A statement by Mr. Paul Harling, Director of the United Nations High Commission, said: "In spite of the overall decrease of the number of refugees... the barbarous atrocities inflicted by the Thai pirates have never diminished."[12]

While most of the attention has been focused on the great ordeals and misadventures of the boat people, there have been people who did not use boats or jets to escape from communist Vietnam. They are called land people, who crossed the border of Vietnam, walking through the wild-beast and poisonous-reptile-infested jungles of Cambodia facing uncountable risks and perilous circumstances. Many died along the way. Those refugees who managed to get to Thailand were eventually put in concentration' camps or holding camps until their resettlement in a third country could be processed.

As to the acceptance of the Vietnamese refugees to other countries, the degrees in attitude have changed. Immediately after the fall of Saigon in Spring, 1975, the escapees were first warmly welcomed by neighboring governments, but eventually as the numbers of refugees increased, their arrivals created economic burdens upon those governments, which accordingly changed their attitudes and policies.

For example, the Malaysian navy set up a blockade to keep the Vietnamese boat-people out of their waters. The refugees who succeded in getting ashore were forced into barbed-wire pens and herded into broken-down fishing boats then towed

[10]*"Cong Dong" (The Community), Houston, Texas, November 1984, p. 18.*
[11]*Dennis D. Gray, "Jumbo Jet Refugees from Vietnam are Quietly Gaining on Boat People," Houston Chronicle, 21 December 1983, p.3*
[12]*"New York Times," July 6, 1984.*

back to sea, with little fuel or water and almost no chance of surviving.

In late December in 1978 a large shipload of refugees arrived in Manila Harbor in the Philippines. The ship was too heavy to be towed back out to sea and there wasn't room for the 2,200 people on board to be kept in barbed-wire pens. So the Philippines government let the ship sit there for two months. Sanitation problems were horrendous. The people's torment was unimaginable. Hundreds of refugees were so crowded on the deck of the boat that some had to hang from the masts.

Fortunately the United Nations Refugees Commission came to the help of the refugees with financial subsidies. However, 1982 through 1983 were the years of economic recessions in most countries throughout the world and subsidies had to be substantially reduced. The United States Government tried its best to offer assistance especially in the years 1976-1979, but as of 1980 to the present, the resettlement or refugee policy of the U.S. Government has changed not only in financial contributions but has now imposed more restrictions in admitting additional refugees into this country by categorizing the latter into two groups — political refugees and economic refugees.[13]

By political it means those who have had to flee from Vietnam because of reasons such as persecution, political imprisonment and other such nature. If they are categorized as economic refugees, they will be refused admission into the U.S.

For instance, upon arrival in Thailand the refugees were asked if they had come to Thailand because they were short of food. If they answered yes, they would be classified by I.N.S.

[13]U.S. Department of Health and Human Services, Refugee Resettlement Program, Report to Congress (Washington, D.C.; 31 January 1984), p. 4.

(Immigration and Naturalization Service) as "economic immigrants" rather than "political refugees," and denied resettlement in the U.S. even if they already had families in the U.S. In the year 1979, I.N.S. rejected 7,000 people on this basis, though the State Department had already approved.[14]

Most of the time, the refugees "because of language barrier" could not express themselves clearly enough during the interviews, and the regrettable consequence was that they were refused political status. If we were to consider the refugee problem or the immigrants on a wider scope   no one can deny the fact that most if not all who came to the U.S. were in one way or another primarily economic refugees rather than political refugees. For instance the Irish immigrants, the Italians, the Japanese and so forth mainly came to this country as economic immigrants. So, why is it that now there is discrimination against the Vietnamese refugees when they have been risking their lives daily in order to escape from the communist regime?

Since fewer and fewer refugees from Southeast Asia are processed favorably as political immigrants, many Vietnamese families now residing in the U.S. as well as in other free countries eagerly look forward to newly effective measures to be adopted by the United States' Government and communist Vietnam in the near future so as to enable them to be reunited with their relatives. This is undeniably in conformity to humanitarian criteria.

As of 1983 there are more than 175,000 Vietnamese, Cambodians and Laotians in refugee camps in Southeast Asia. Most of them are in Hong Kong, locked up in prison camps in unheated dormitories holding up to 250 people in the equivalent of small metallic cages vertically stacked.[15] Some

[14]William Shawcross, "Southeast Asia's Camps of Misery," *World Press Review,* September 1983, p. 33.

[15]William Shawcross, "Southeast Asia's Camps of Misery," *World Press Review,* September 1983, p. 33.

refugees have been living in camps for 3-4 years without knowing where to go. The situation is becoming more and more gloomy for those miserable people.

At the time of this writing there are hundreds of thousands of Vietnamese in Vietnam who have been approved by the U.S. authorities to be admitted into the U.S. for reunification with their families, but communist authorities still detain these people and prevent the issuance of exit-visas. Officially one and a half million have applied to leave Vietnam for the U.S., and once they have done so, they would lose employment and their food rationing privileges in their native country.

The Vietnamese someday hope to return to their homeland as they have done so many times before, just like the Jewish people who have been returning to their ancestors' homeland. Until then they will respectfully consider their second home the U.S. or other free countries where they have been settled. They enjoy the pride of being free Vietnamese in America, even the freedom of going into business for oneself and the freedom to succeed or fail. In the following pages we shall discuss the transitional era that the Vietnamese have gone through during their first decade of resettlement in the U.S.A.

S U M M A R Y
REFUGEE ARRIVALS IN THE UNITED STATES

(prepared by J. Lawrence RP/EX ext. 21315)
Report Date : November 18, 1983

| AREA | FY-75 | FY-76 | FY-77 | FY-78 | FY-79 | FY-80 | FY-81 | FY-82 | FY-83 | FY-84 | FY-85 | FY-86 | TOTAL | REMARKS |
|---|---|---|---|---|---|---|---|---|---|---|---|---|---|
| AFRICA | - | - | - | - | - | 955 | 2,119 | 3,326 | 2,648 | - | - | - | 9,048 | |
| ASIA | 135,000 | 15,000 | 7,000 | 20,574 | 76,521 | 163,799 | 131,139 | 73,522 | 39,408 | - | - | - | 661,963 | |
| EASTERN EUROPE | 1,947 | 1,756 | 1,755 | 2,245 | 3,393 | 5,025 | 6,704 | 10,780 | 12,083 | - | - | - | 45,688 | |
| SOVIET UNION | 6,211 | 7,450 | 8,191 | 10,688 | 24,449 | 28,444 | 13,444 | 2,756 | 1,409 | - | - | - | 103,042 | |
| LATIN AMERICA | 3,000 | 3,000 | 3,000 | 3,000 | 7,000 | 6,662 | 2,017 | 602 | 668 | - | - | - | 28,949 | |
| NEAR EAST | - | - | - | - | - | 2,231 | 3,829 | 6,369 | 5,465 | - | - | - | 17,894 | |
| TOTAL | 146,158 | 27,206 | 19,946 | 36,507 | 111,363 | 207,116 | 159,252 | 97,355 | 61,681 | - | - | - | 866,584 | |

1907A

Acknowledgement: Tables and reports reproduced in the ensuing pages are extracted from "REPORTS TO THE CONGRESS", January 31, 1983 & 1984, submitted by the Refugee Resettlement Program, U.S. Department of Health and Human Services, Social Security Administration, Office of Refugee Resettlement.

REFUGEE ARRIVALS IN THE UNITED STATES
FY 1983

(prepared by J. Lawrence RP/EX ext. 21315)
Report Date: November 18, 1983

| AREA | OCT | NOV | DEC | JAN | FEB | MAR | APR | MAY | JUN | JUL | AUG | SEP | TOTAL | CONSULTATION |
|---|---|---|---|---|---|---|---|---|---|---|---|---|---|---|
| AFRICA | 9 | 227 | 221 | 39 | 98 | 151 | 154 | 153 | 176 | 99 | 312 | 959* | 2,648* | 3,000 |
| EAST ASIA | 1,359 | 3,081 | 2,622 | 2,637 | 2,053 | 3,047 | 2,996 | 2,950 | 4,301 | 3,628 | 4,953 | 5,781 | 39,408 | 64,000 |
| EASTERN EUROPE AND SOVIET UNION | 405 | 1,357 | 1,361 | 812 | 1,028 | 1,484 | 957 | 1,134 | 1,474 | 1,042 | 1,079 | 1,359 | 13,492 | 15,000 |
| LATIN AMERICA AND CARIBBEAN | 0 | 4 | 0 | 0 | 6 | 0 | 11 | 0 | 57 | 208 | 340 | 42+ | 668+ | 2,000 |
| NEAR EAST AND SOUTH ASIA | 114 | 185 | 365 | 338 | 215 | 356 | 274 | 584 | 1,174 | 310 | 364 | 1,186** | 5,465** | 6,000 |
| TOTAL | 1,887 | 4,854 | 4,569 | 3,876 | 3,400 | 5,038 | 4,392 | 4,821 | 7,182 | 5,287 | 7,048 | 9,327 | 61,681 | 90,000 |

* AFRICA

| Processed in Europe: | SEP | YEAR TO DATE |
|---|---|---|
| Ethiopians | 12 | 185 |
| Angolans | 1 | 1 |
| Mozambicans | 4 | 4 |
| Namibians | — | 1 |
|  | 17 | 191 |
| Processed in Africa: |  |  |
| Ethiopians | 942 | 2,149 |
| Mozambicans | 0 | 7 |
| South Africans | 0 | 9 |
| Namibians | 0 | 0 |
| Zairians | 0 | 11 |
| Malawis | 0 | 1 |
| Angolans | 0 | 9 |
|  | 942 | 2,457 |
| T O T A L : | 959 | 2,648 |

** NEAR EAST & SOUTH ASIA

| Processed in Europe: | SEP | YEAR TO DATE |
|---|---|---|
| Afghans | 45 | 651 |
| Iraqis | 74 | 1,583 |
| Iranians | 464 | 947 |
| Syrians | 0 | 9 |
|  | 583 | 3,190 |
| Processed in Africa: |  |  |
| Afghans | 0 | 6 |
| Processed in South Asia: |  |  |
| Afghans | 603 | 2,269 |
| T O T A L : | 1,186 | 5,465 |

+ LATIN AMERICA & CARIBBEAN

| Processed in Europe: | SEP | YEAR TO DATE |
|---|---|---|
| Cubans | 10 | 106 |
| Processed in Latin America: |  |  |
| Cubans | 32 | 560 |
| Argentines | 0 | 2 |
| T O T A L : | 42 | 668 |

OFFICE OF REFUGEE RESETTLEMENT
DEPARTMENT OF HEALTH AND HUMAN SERVICES

SOUTHEAST ASIAN REFUGEES: ESTIMATED CUMULATIVE STATE POPULATIONS a/
INCLUDING ENTRIES FROM 1975 THROUGH 1/31/84

Note: New adjustments for secondary migration were incorporated into these
estimates as of 9/30/83.

| STATE OF RESIDENCE | ESTIMATED TOTAL | STATE OF RESIDENCE | ESTIMATED TOTAL |
|---|---|---|---|
| ALABAMA | 2,400 | NEVADA | 2,000 |
| ALASKA | 200 | NEW HAMPSHIRE | 600 |
| ARIZONA | 4,900 | NEW JERSEY | 6,000 |
| ARKANSAS | 2,900 | NEW MEXICO | 2,500 |
| CALIFORNIA | 248,900 | NEW YORK | 23,300 |
| COLORADO | 10,200 | NORTH CAROLINA | 4,900 |
| CONNECTICUT | 6,200 | NORTH DAKOTA | 900 |
| DELAWARE | 300 | OHIO | 10,000 |
| DISTRICT OF COLUMBIA | 1,200 | OKLAHOMA | 8,700 |
| FLORIDA | 11,900 | OREGON | 16,500 |
| GEORGIA | 8,100 | PENNSYLVANIA | 23,400 |
| HAWAII | 6,900 | RHODE ISLAND | 6,300 |
| IDAHO | 1,400 | SOUTH CAROLINA | 2,400 |
| ILLINOIS | 24,000 | SOUTH DAKOTA | 1,000 |
| INDIANA | 4,300 | TENNESSEE | 4,200 |
| IOWA | 8,300 | TEXAS | 54,900 |
| KANSAS | 8,900 | UTAH | 8,200 |
| KENTUCKY | 2,400 | VERMONT | 600 |
| LOUISIANA | 13,600 | VIRGINIA | 20,700 |
| MAINE | 1,400 | WASHINGTON | 31,000 |
| MARYLAND | 7,600 | WEST VIRGINIA | 500 |
| MASSACHUSETTS | 15,900 | WISCONSIN | 9,700 |
| MICHIGAN | 10,100 | WYOMING | 300 |
| MINNESOTA | 21,500 | GUAM | 200 |
| MISSISSIPPI | 1,500 | OTHER TERRITORIES | b/ |
| MISSOURI | 6,400 | | |
| MONTANA | 1,000 | | |
| NEBRASKA | 2,300 | | |

TOTAL    673,500

a/    Adjusted for secondary migration through 9/30/83, rounded to the nearest hundred.

b/    Fewer than 100.

Estimated Southeast Asian Refugee Population by State
September 30, 1982 and September 30, 1983ª/

| State | 9/30/82 Number | Percent | 9/30/83 Number | Percen |
|---|---|---|---|---|
| Alabama | 2,200 | 0.4% | 2,300 | 0.4° |
| Alaska | 300 | c/ | 200 | c/ |
| Arizona | 3,700 | 0.6 | 4,600 | 0.7 |
| Arkansas | 2,900 | 0.5 | 2,900 | 0.4 |
| California | 225,500 | 36.4 | 244,100 | 37.1 |
| Colorado | 10,500 | 1.7 | 10,100 | 1.5 |
| Connecticut | 6,300 | 1.0 | 6,000 | 0.9 |
| Delaware | 300 | c/ | 300 | c/ |
| District of Columbia | 1,000 | 0.2 | 1,000 | 0.2 |
| Florida | 10,400 | 1.7 | 11,700 | 1.8 |
| Georgia | 5,500 | 0.9 | 7,800 | 1.2 |
| Hawaii | 5,600 | 0.9 | 6,800 | 1.0 |
| Idaho | 1,300 | 0.2 | 1,300 | 0.2 |
| Illinois | 21,700 | 3.5 | 23,500 | 3.6 |
| Indiana | 4,100 | 0.7 | 4,200 | 0.6 |
| Iowa | 8,100 | 1.3 | 8,100 | 1.2 |
| Kansas | 9,100 | 1.5 | 8,700 | 1.3 |
| Kentucky | 2,600 | 0.4 | 2,300 | 0.4 |
| Louisiana | 15,100 | 2.4 | 13,300 | 2.0 |
| Maine | 1,100 | 0.2 | 1,300 | 0.2 |
| Maryland | 7,600 | 1.2 | 7,300 | 1.1 |
| Massachusetts | 12,000 | 1.9 | 15,400 | 2.3 |
| Michigan | 9,500 | 1.5 | 10,000 | 1.5 |
| Minnesota | 21,200 | 3.4 | 21,000 | 3.2 |
| Mississippi | 1,400 | 0.2 | 1,500 | 0.2 |
| Missouri | 5,300 | 0.9 | 6,200 | 0.9 |
| Montana | 1,000 | 0.2 | 1,000 | 0.2 |
| Nebraska | 2,300 | 0.4 | 2,300 | 0.3 |
| Nevada | 1,800 | 0.3 | 1,900 | 0.3 |
| New Hampshire | 400 | c/ | 600 | c/ |
| New Jersey | 5,200 | 0.8 | 5,900 | 0.9 |
| New Mexico | 2,700 | 0.4 | 2,400 | 0.4 |
| New York | 18,300 | 3.0 | 22,700 | 3.4 |
| North Carolina | 4,000 | 0.6 | 4,800 | 0.7 |
| North Dakota | 700 | 0.1 | 800 | 0.1 |
| Ohio | 8,800 | 1.4 | 9,800 | 1.5 |
| Oklahoma | 9,100 | 1.5 | 8,500 | 1.3 |
| Oregon | 17,800 | 2.9 | 16,200 | 2.5 |
| Pennsylvania | 23,200 | 3.7 | 23,000 | 3.5 |
| Rhode Island | 6,000 | 1.0 | 6,200 | 0.9 |
| South Carolina | 2,100 | 0.3 | 2,400 | 0.4 |
| South Dakota | 1,000 | 0.2 | 1,000 | 0.2 |
| Tennessee | 4,200 | 0.7 | 4,100 | 0.6 |
| Texas | 50,700 | 8.2 | 53,600 | 8.1 |
| Utah | 7,200 | 1.2 | 7,900 | 1.2 |

| State | 9/30/82 | | 9/30/83 | |
|---|---|---|---|---|
| | Number | Percent | Number | Percent |
| Vermont | 400 | c/ | 500 | c/ |
| Virginia | 19,600 | 3.2 | 20,300 | 3.1 |
| Washington | 29,900 | 4.8 | 30,400 | 4.6 |
| West Virginia | 400 | c/ | 500 | c/ |
| Wisconsin | 7,900 | 1.3 | 9,600 | 1.5 |
| Wyoming | 300 | c/ | 300 | c/ |
| Guam | 200 | c/ | 200 | c/ |
| Other Territories | b/ | c/ | b/ | c/ |
| TOTAL | 619,800 | 100.0% | 659,000 | 100.0% |

a/The September 1982 estimates were constructed by taking the January
1981 INS alien registration, adjusting it for underregistration, adding
persons who arrived from January 1981 through September 1982, and
adjusting the totals so derived for secondary migration. The September
1983 estimates were constructed similarly by using the known distribution
of the population in January 1981, adding arrivals from January 1981
through September 1983, and adjusting those totals for secondary
migration. Estimates of secondary migration rates were developed from
data submitted by the States. Figures are rounded to the nearest hundred
and may not add to totals due to rounding.

b/ Less than 50.

c/ Less than 0.1 percent.

TABLE 10

Secondary Migration Data Compiled from the Refugee State-of-Origin
Report:  June 30, 1983[a/]

| State | Non-Movers | Out-Migrants | In-Migrants | Net Migration |
|---|---|---|---|---|
| Alabama | 91 | 419 | 43 | -376 |
| Alaska b/ | 0 | 169 | 0 | -169 |
| Arizona | 173 | 595 | 62 | -533 |
| Arkansas | 107 | 317 | 50 | -267 |
| California | 66,620 | 1,431 | 23,977 | 22,546 |
| Colorado | 1,227 | 758 | 432 | -326 |
| Connecticut | 510 | 388 | 158 | -230 |
| Delaware | 23 | 25 | 5 | -20 |
| District of Columbia | 198 | 1,154 | 16 | -1,138 |
| Florida | 1,361 | 1,195 | 377 | -818 |
| Georgia | 853 | 998 | 159 | -839 |
| Hawaii | 1,516 | 431 | 184 | -247 |
| Idaho | 142 | 201 | 38 | -163 |
| Illinois d/ | 2,924 | 1,991 | 449 | -1,542 |
| Indiana | 126 | 337 | 8 | -329 |
| Iowa | 832 | 477 | 154 | -323 |
| Kansas | 1,060 | 652 | 389 | -263 |
| Kentucky | 263 | 530 | 0 | -530 |
| Louisiana | 973 | 639 | 339 | -300 |
| Maine | 194 | 78 | 21 | -57 |
| Maryland | 398 | 528 | 512 | -16 |
| Massachusetts | 5,254 | 840 | 1,418 | 578 |
| Michigan | 1,829 | 652 | 391 | -261 |
| Minnesota | 4,573 | 1,400 | 1,007 | -393 |
| Mississippi | 95 | 166 | 104 | -62 |
| Missouri | 1,465 | 779 | 245 | -534 |
| Montana | 50 | 49 | 13 | -36 |
| Nebraska | 236 | 388 | 41 | -347 |
| Nevada | 162 | 217 | 15 | -202 |
| New Hampshire | 68 | 63 | 11 | -52 |
| New Jersey | 1,145 | 475 | 247 | -228 |
| New Mexico | 272 | 527 | 67 | -460 |
| New York | d/ | 2,073 | 820 | -1,253 |
| North Carolina | 207 | 421 | 45 | -376 |
| North Dakota | 221 | 103 | 36 | -67 |
| Ohio | 1,332 | 818 | 212 | -606 |
| Oklahoma | 452 | 633 | 137 | -496 |
| Oregon | 3,002 | 1,939 | 662 | -1,277 |
| Pennsylvania | c/ | 1,389 | c/ | -1,389 |
| Rhode Island | 740 | 286 | 540 | 254 |
| South Carolina | 103 | 292 | 5 | -287 |
| South Dakota | 90 | 124 | 10 | -114 |
| Tennessee | 263 | 573 | 31 | -542 |
| Texas | 3,509 | 4,733 | 1,300 | -3,433 |
| Utah | 836 | 860 | 207 | -653 |

| State | Non-Movers | Out-Migrants | In-Migrants | Net Migration |
|---|---|---|---|---|
| Vermont | 87 | 37 | 34 | -3 |
| Virginia | 2,413 | 934 | 1,364 | 430 |
| Washington | 5,844 | 1,925 | 1,744 | -181 |
| West Virginia | 43 | 59 | 1 | -58 |
| Wisconsin | 1,185 | 341 | 411 | 70 |
| Wyoming | 20 | 40 | 15 | -25 |
| Guam | 28 | 1,875 | 0 | -1,875 |
| Other b/ | 0 | 182 | 0 | -182 |
| TOTAL | 115,115 | 38,506 | 38,506 | 0 |

a/ This table represents a compilation of data reported by the States on Form ORR-11. The population base is refugees receiving State-administered services on 6/30/83. Persons without social security numbers were dropped from the analysis. Secondary migration is defined as residence on the reporting date in a State other than that of initial placements. With regard to a selected State, out-migrants are persons initially placed there who were living elsewhere on the reporting date, and in-migrants are persons living there on the reporting date who were initially placed elsewhere. "Non-movers" are persons who, on the reporting date, were living in their initial State of placement; it is recognized that individuals could have moved out of, and back to, their initial State between their original placement and the reporting date.

b/ Not participating in the refugee program.

c/ State did not submit a report.

d/ State was not able to report on its entire caseload.

TABLE

Refugee Arrivals in the United States by Month:
FY 1983

| Month | Number of Arrivals | | |
|---|---|---|---|
| | Southeast Asians | All Others | Total |
| October | 1,356 | 439 | 1,795 |
| November | 3,080 | 1,655 | 4,735 |
| December | 2,619 | 1,868 | 4,487 |
| January | 2,637 | 1,199 | 3,836 |
| February | 2,064 | 1,313 | 3,377 |
| March | 3,001 | 1,920 | 4,921 |
| April | 3,035 | 1,296 | 4,331 |
| May | 2,970 | 1,830 | 4,800 |
| June | 4,284 | 2,840 | 7,124 |
| July | 3,345 | 1,536 | 4,881 |
| August | 4,986 | 2,028 | 7,014 |
| September | 5,790 | 3,571 | 9,361 |
| TOTAL | 39,167 | 21,495 | 60,662 |

FY 1983: October 1, 1982--September 30, 1983.

TABLE

Southeast Asian Refugee Arrivals by State of Initial Resettlement:
FY 1983

## Country of Citizenship

| State | Cambodia | Laos | Vietnam | Total |
|-------|----------|------|---------|-------|
| Alabama | 92 | 6 | 76 | 174 |
| Alaska | 0 | 9 | 9 | 18 |
| Arizona | 250 | 6 | 751 | 1,007 |
| Arkansas | 16 | 23 | 71 | 110 |
| California | 2,733 | 832 | 7,791 | 11,356 |
| | | | | |
| Colorado | 135 | 14 | 286 | 435 |
| Connecticut | 204 | 52 | 136 | 392 |
| Delaware | 0 | 0 | 2 | 2 |
| District of Columbia | 100 | 40 | 195 | 335 |
| Florida | 214 | 32 | 527 | 773 |
| | | | | |
| Georgia | 286 | 24 | 432 | 742 |
| Hawaii | 16 | 51 | 266 | 333 |
| Idaho | 21 | 19 | 25 | 65 |
| Illinois | 554 | 195 | 570 | 1,319 |
| Indiana | 19 | 23 | 93 | 135 |
| | | | | |
| Iowa | 90 | 65 | 115 | 270 |
| Kansas | 75 | 34 | 396 | 505 |
| Kentucky | 64 | 9 | 53 | 126 |
| Louisiana | 124 | 43 | 637 | 804 |
| Maine | 99 | 6 | 33 | 138 |
| | | | | |
| Maryland | 232 | 45 | 294 | 571 |
| Massachusetts | 945 | 61 | 736 | 1,742 |
| Michigan | 34 | 26 | 241 | 301 |
| Minnesota | 543 | 128 | 650 | 1,321 |
| Mississippi | 0 | 0 | 87 | 87 |
| | | | | |
| Missouri | 100 | 43 | 251 | 394 |
| Montana | 6 | 18 | 4 | 28 |
| Nebraska | 21 | 8 | 60 | 89 |
| Nevada | 40 | 17 | 113 | 170 |
| New Hampshire | 110 | 1 | 10 | 121 |
| | | | | |
| New Jersey | 34 | 16 | 365 | 415 |
| New Mexico | 33 | 14 | 96 | 143 |
| New York | 710 | 55 | 1,102 | 1,867 |
| North Carolina | 590 | 8 | 146 | 744 |
| North Dakota | 19 | 7 | 8 | 34 |

## THE NEW LIFE OF OVERSEAS VIETNAMESE

So swiftly the first ten years have gone by. The overseas Vietnamese have experienced much hardship and suffering while settling in free countries that have admitted them and offered them asylum to re-start their lives. They have had to take refuge in friendly lands so as to avoid living under a totalitarian regime considered to be one of the most atrocious ever witnessed by the free democratic world. Very often when people are forced into a dead-end they will find out new means for survival. That is exactly the case of hundreds of thousands of Vietnamese refugees who had to take flight from their native country.

Many other ethnic minority groups in the United States feel surprised at the rapid social and economic recoveries of the Vietnamese newcomers. The former sometimes wonder that either the Vietnamese refugees managed to bring with them quite a bit of wealth or they might have been specially favored by the local authorities in resettlement assistance. The reality was absolutely not so. Only a very small number of corrupt officials and dishonest businessmen ("affairistes") of the defunct Thieu regime succeeded in bringing with them part of the deceitfully acquired fortunes; other than that, the great majority of refugees came to this country in extremely miserable conditions leaving almost everything behind. The fact that they got out of "hell" was considered indeed quite fortunate. As for the U.S. Government, it had envisaged and appropriated the necessary fund to assist an estimated number of 150,000 refugees in the first contingents that came here in the second quarter of 1975. It turned out that about 140,000 Indochinese were later officially announced to be the figure of escapees rescued by U.S. military planes and naval vessels.

# THE DEAD END

When forced into a dead-end, man has the instinct to exert his utmost to think out means of survival. That is the circumstance compelling him to put out his greatest physical and mental strength and probe deeply into his mind to think of the best ways and means to survive. It was mainly due to the ultimate efforts and also to the intelligence to react and the adaptability to new conditions that helped the Vietnamese refugees confront such colossal trials and challenges in their first days and months of resettlement in the U.S.A.

The Vietnamese newcomers had manifested their courage and sprightliness to their hosts and other minority groups in each and every locality they first set foot on. They were also determined to rebuild their lives from scratch: all over the United States up to Canada, as well as in several European countries and down to Australia and New Zealand. Through the first decade of trials, the Vietnamese expatriates, with their sweat and blood, have proven to the Free World that they are second to none as far as pioneering spirit is concerned. Their determination to be self-sufficient and successful in the new lands has won the praise of those around them. And today, they are proud to be contributing a small part to the cultural activities and economic as well as industrial developments of this great nation, even though at this stage their share is still very modest. Nevertheless, they have overcome most of the odds against them in such a short period of time — the first decade of survival in foreign lands in search of Freedom and Justice.

In a way, it could be said that after the first ten years overseas, the Vietnamese newcomers have succeeded in establishing a relatively strong social infrastructure upon which they can build other more ambitious projects for the second decade which hopefully should be more successful and significant than the initial decade. Looking into the future, the Vietnamese expatriates realize that they will have to exert greater efforts and contribute more energy in order to attain meaningful results. All that has been achieved so far has been based mainly on hard work and their "old" ways of doing things. Undeniably this is insufficient and inappropriate to compete effectively in a technologically advanced nation such as the United States. Consequently, the Vietnamese newcomers must acquire new knowledge in all fields of activities, especially in economic, financial, industrial and technological discipline so as to keep pace with their American brothers. The younger generations of Vietnamese in this land must not spare any efforts to improve on their knowledge by taking advantage of the plentiful facilities readily available in the great numbers of academic and technical institutes. If the Vietnamese Americans do not make further and greater progress in all branches of studies in the years to come, they will become second class citizens and have to bear the inevitable dire consequences.

## TRADITIONAL SKILLS versus MODERN SKILLS

Skills among the Vietnamese residents can be divided into two main categories: traditional or "old" skills comprise those brought over from their native country, such as running family restaurants, grocery stores, street-corner drugstores, ... manufacturing daily necessaries (sweaters, socks, stockings, shirts, food items, confectionery...), lacquer works, silverware, copperware, and so forth; while the "modern" or "new" skills are those they have been learning since their arrival in this country, such as: managing convenience stores, washaterias, liquor stores, pizza parlors, one-hour photo labs; acquiring new knowledge such as: modern business administration, advanced sciences, computer science, real estate, insurance brokerage, investments on the exchanges, running video stores, etc.[1]

Oriental grocery stores, confectioneries, Vietnamese rice noodle soup shops, and the like, can build up immediate clientele, but similar outfits will also pop up like mushrooms, and it will not take long before the limited market is saturated. At that point, competition will certainly be very acute, and as a consequence, a considerable number of business will go broke.

Of all the professions brought over from Vietnam, the medical professions seem to be the most lucrative. Because of the prolonged War, the Military Medical Corps (of the Republic of Vietnam) had turned out quite a few physicians, dentists and pharmacists in response to the urgent demand of the various and numerous combat units in the field. With the termination of the fighting, these military medical practitioners also fled to the U.S. After some brush-up courses and basic tests, they were subsequently licensed by the state boards to practice their profession. Due to the language barrier especially, they immediately drew in a great number of Vietnamese clients, who were mostly covered by Medicare and Medicaid.[2] So far the medical professionals are second to none in term of income. They will not come across any competition till the next crop of Vietnamese medical graduates from American colleges who will supply the market in earnest in three or four more years.

Fishing and shrimping is also among the few professions that can be continued once the professionals are ready to return to sea for their catches. They are considered the very fortunate ones, second perhaps only to the medical

---

[1] Refer to Chapter 3, p. 105.
[2] Refer to Chapter 3, p. 105.

professionals as far as revenues are concerned.

The publishing business is limited to only a few entrepreneurs who know the ins and outs of the trade due to its technical and marketing complexities. However, the number of first-time publishers of Vietnamese books and periodicals has increased in the recent couple of years (as of 1982) and it is hoped that they can contribute effectively to the popularization of Vietnamese culture among the Vietnamese communities.

One peculiarity in a free-press society such as the United States, observed through a recent survey, is that the number of Vietnamese-language newspapers and periodicals has increased by leaps and bounds to the extent that in Orange County (California) alone, there are currently seventeen such publications which are handed out free of charge. This phenomenon is due to the fact that most of them are ad tabloids supported sometimes voluntarily by local businessmen and the medical professionals, but also sometimes through some forms of pressure. In Houston (Texas), with a Vietnamese population of approximately 50,000 there are already nine such papers and magazines. The circulation may range from 500 copies to as many as 3000 copies per issue, and it is needless to say, the editorial quality is another matter that is not relevant to this study.

Anyway, the author has a personal viewpoint in regard to the abundance of newspapers advocated by such a number of enthusiasts because he believes that the more printed words are spread out to the residents in the communities the better it is for the preservation of Vietnamese culture, especially for the permanent existence of the Vietnamese language in this country. Of course, as time goes by, those publications of inferior quality will be eliminated through the ultimate judgment of the readers.

All in all, it will soon be an accepted fact that traditional or modern skills and trades will need adequate renovation and updating in good management in order to survive in this competitive society. Even an oriental medicinal herbal store will have to apply modern business administrative techniques so as to keep itself afloat in this sharply competitive environment, if not, it will go under due to high pressure from enterprising competitors in the neighborhood. It is fair competition that makes the free enterprise system work so efficiently in this capitalistic country. Consequently, conservative and especially old-fashioned and outdated businesses have little or no chance to survive in the existing business surroundings.

Superannuated outfits will have to be renovated with modern business management. For example, running a restaurant in the traditional way, even with its outstanding cuisine, is no match for an outfit that has superb decor, good management, excellent service, fair prices, outstanding chefs, and modern marketing gimmicks!

Another essential point that deserves the scrutiny of the prospective entrepreneur is: Which would be more advantageous to the business: to cater to only .3% of the population or to the 100% of people in his locality? Watch how some Mexican dishes are now being Americanized and marketed through fast food chains, how the varieties of pizzas are being sold all over the states, the operation of certain well-known English fried fish stores... What successes they have obtained through the "mass" clientele! With the same kind of capital outlay, the Vietnamese entrepreneurs should think of the general U.S. market rather than the limited Vietnamese market. A well-organized convenience store is naturally more promising than an oriental grocery store (started up with equal funding). Statistics have proven this point again and again.

## ASSIMILATION INTO THE MAINSTREAM

A considerable number of Vietnamese newcomers were ex-servicemen who had spent most of their lifetime in combatting communist aggressors. When they arrived in the new land, deprived of all professional and artistic skills, they were the most handicapped among the refugees. However, thanks to their energetic endeavors, courage and diligence, they started learning new trades as circumstances permitted and overcame the language barrier in record time so as to communicate with local people. They set invaluable examples of endurance to their fellow countrypeople and instilled inspiration on all those around them by their patience and stoicism, representative of a new breed of pioneers. Some willingly accepted menial but honest jobs to earn their living such as: helping at gas stations, managing motels or apartment complexes, car-washing, truck-driving, house painting, helping at construction sites... Only one or two years after, they could save up enough capital to start workshops of their own.

The assimilation of Vietnamese residents into the American mainstream of life in such record time amazed quite a few local people, but if the latter had observed how arduously those people worked and what determination they had in restructuring their lives in their newly adopted homeland, the local people would easily understand why the new settlers attained their goals in such a short lapse of time.

## COMPARED WITH OTHER MINORITY GROUPS

The United States is a gigantic melting-pot of so many racial groups coming from all over the world. This is the land of refugees and immigrants, and all knowledgeable Americans are aware of that fact. With the exception of the native American Indians, all other racial groups have migrated to this land in search of freedom, taking asylum from political or religious persecutions, or solving their social and economic problems.

Words of praise have been lavished on other ethnic groups including the Chinese, Japanese, Jews, Koreans... for their enterprising spirits while settling in this country. The Vietnamese immigrants should imitate the good points set out by their predecessors and shun the bad points. They should learn from past lessons and costly experiences of the forerunners who already paved the way during the past hundred years.

## ABILITIES OF THE VIETNAMESE

No one can deny the fact that the Vietnamese have learned much from Chinese culture due to the long years of domination. The Vietnamese learned quite a few good things from the Chinese and this is no shame to acknowledge, for even European nations have learned from one another so many things over the centuries. In fact, the spread of cultures has contributed considerably to the advance of civilization.

The Vietnamese learned from the Chinese, but the characteriestic is that very often the former could improve on the knowledge acquired. The Chinese introduced to the Vietnamese their language and writing, but when the

Vietnamese learned the new language, they would pronounce the words according to Vietnamese ways and they even based on the Chinese writing to invent their own system of writing called "nôm" characters that only the Vietnamese could understand. Thus, the Vietnamese could read and understand all the books published by the Chinese while very few Chinese intellectuals could understand the "nôm" writing.

As for handicrafts, the Vietnamese also learned them from the Chinese conquerors and neighbors, but all arts connoisseurs must agree that in numerous artifacts such as: silverware, copperware, sculptures, silk weaving, lacquer works, inlaying of mother-of-pearls, etc. the Vietnamese have often proven to be superior in craftsmanship and artistic taste. There are numerous other domains in which the learners have, in the long run, proven they could excel their teachers.

This aims at emphasizing on a particular point that the Vietnamese are hardworking and intelligent and can adapt themselves to new circumstances perhaps more quickly than some other people. With those potentials and abilities in a land of opportunity and equality to all, the Vietnamese resettlers can feel comfortable and optimistic for their future by improving on their knowledge and by inspiring their children to advance in their academic and technological achievements. The American hosts can feel assured that the Vietnamese newcomers - who eventually will become Vietnamese Americans with their well-founded culture and resourceful energy - can be an asset to this nation.

TABLE

**Southeast Asian Refugee Arrivals in the United States
1975 through September 30, 1983**

| | |
|---|---|
| Resettled under Special Parole Program (1975) | 129,792 |
| Resettled under Humanitarian Parole Program (1975) | 602 |
| Resettled under Special Lao Program (1976) | 3,466 |
| Resettled under Expanded Parole Program (1976) | 11,000 |
| Resettled under "Boat Cases" Program as of August 1, 1977 | 1,883 |

Resettled under Indochinese Parole Programs:

| | |
|---|---|
| August 1, 1977 - September 30, 1977 | 680 |
| October 1, 1977 - September 30, 1978 | 20,397 |
| October 1, 1978 - September 30, 1979 | 80,678 |
| October 1, 1979 - September 30, 1980 | 166,727 |

Resettled under Refugee Act of 1980:

| | |
|---|---|
| October 1, 1980 - September 30, 1981 | 132,454 |
| October 1, 1981 - September 30, 1982 | 72,155 |
| October 1, 1982 - September 30, 1983 | 39,167 |
| TOTAL: | 659,001 |

Prior to the passage of the Refugee Act of 1980, most Southeast Asian refugees entered the United States as "parolees" (refugees) under a series of parole authorization granted by the Attorney General under the Immigration and Nationality Act. These parole authorizations are usually identified by the terms used in this table.

## Current Employment Status of Southeast Asian Refugees

| Year of Entry | labor force participation | | unemployment | |
|---|---|---|---|---|
| | In 1982 | In 1983 | In 1982 | In 1983 |
| 1983 | -- | 20.7% | -- | 55.0% |
| 1982 | 25.2% | 40.9% | 62.5% | 30.4% |
| 1981 | 41.5% | 46.5% | 40.7% | 16.8% |
| 1980 | 51.3% | 55.3% | 32.1% | 21.1% |
| 1979 | 60.2% | 60.5% | 19.3% | 17.8% |
| 1978 | 67.6% | 68.2% | 19.0% | 19.7% |
| 1976-7 | 74.3% | 79.5% | 9.4% | 17.2% |
| 1975 | 72.1% | 69.7% | 12.7% | 12.1% |
| U.S. rates* | 64.1% | 64.1% | 9.9% | 8.4% |

* October unadjusted figures from the Bureau of Labor Statistics, Department of Labor.

The kinds of jobs that refugees find in the United States generally are of lower status than those they held in their country of origin. For example, 57 per cent of those employed adults sampled had held white collar jobs in their country of origin, but only 27 percent hold similar jobs in the United States. Conversely, far more Southeast Asian refugees hold blue collar or service jobs in the U.S. than they did in their countries of origin. The survey data, for example, indicate a tripling of those in service occupations and of those in semi-skilled blue collar occupations.

### Current and Previous Occupational Status

| Occupation | In country of Origin | In U.S. |
|---|---|---|
| Professional Managerial | 13.2% | 5.4% |
| Sales Clerical | 43.3% | 21.7% |
| (TOTAL WHITE COLLAR) | (56.5%) | (27.1%) |
| Skilled | 12.7% | 21.5% |
| Semi-Skilled | 6.5% | 19.2% |
| Laborers | 2.2% | 8.4% |
| (TOTAL BLUE COLLARS) | (21.4%) | |
| Farmers and Fishers | 15.9% | 1.8% |

### Factors Affecting Employment Status

The ability of Southeast Asian refugees to seek and find employment in the United States is the result of many factors. Some of these involve individual decisions about whether to seek work. As in previous surveys, respondents who were not in the labor force were asked why they were not seeking work. The reasons they gave varied by age and sex, but focused on the demands of family life, health problems, and the decisions to gain training and education preparatory to entering the job market.

For those under the age of 24, the pursuit of education was the overriding concern. For those between the ages of 25 and 44, family needs also became a major concern, and for those over the age of 44, health problems predominated as a reason for not seeking worth.

**Reasons for Not Seeking Employment**

**Percent Citing:**

| Age Group | Limited English | Education | Family Needs | Health |
|-----------|-----------------|-----------|--------------|--------|
| 16-24 | 3.8% | 83.0% | 3.2% | 3.1% |
| 25-34 | 9.8% | 31.5% | 29.3% | 4.1% |
| 35-44 | 15.3% | 28.6% | 22.0% | 7.9% |
| over 44 | 13.8% | 8.9% | 10.4% | 28.7% |

The major current refugee characteristic that influences successful involvement in the labor force is English language competence. As in previous surveys, English proficiency had clear effects on labor force participation, on unemployment rates, and on earnings. For those refugees in the sample who were fluent in English, the labor force participation and unemployment rates were similar to those for the overall United States population. Refugees who spoke no English, however, had a labor force participation rate of only 25 percent and an unemployment rate of 36 percent. Refugees who spoke a little English had a labor force participation rate of 55 percent and an unemployment rate of 23 percent.

## THE FIRST DECADE

One full decade has just passed by since the day when the first group of Vietnamese refugees set foot on the new land to re-start their lives from scratch. Looking back, the newcomers had so many recollections of their early experiences in a land where everything seemed new and strange to them. They had to live through those rigorous years in order to witness the ups and downs in each and every overseas Vietnamese household, the drastic changes in most families, and the transformation imposed on the Vietnamese communities. Those are the facts and events that will remain for a long long time in the memory of the Vietnamese-Americans.

While living in the present, the Vietnamese immigrants should look back into the past - the recent past ten years - so as to review a number of meaningful developments that directly concerned their livelihood in a foreign land. They will realize that this is time to have some sort of self-examination and re-evaluation, and then focus their concentration into the future in order to form a picture of what will be happening to them and to their children in the years to come.

## THE NEW COMMNUNITIES

According to the latest reports, the Vietnamese population in the United States is currently about 588,000 people scattered all over the fifty states. But actually, as the years pass by, partly due to the fact that the expatriates prefer to flock together to form their own communities, and partly on account of the rigid cold climate in some localities, the Vietnamese immigrants have decided to change residence by moving from the northern states to the sunbelt where the climate suits them much more favorably. The current most important Vietnamese communities are found in Orange County, Los Angeles (California), Dallas, Houston (Texas), Seattle (Washington), Denver (Colorado), New Orleans (Louisiana), Arlington (Virginia)...

As the communities expand, social problems also become inevitable. The author has had chancesto talk to local people in the private sectors as well as in administrative agencies. He has come to know that social problems are rather common among other ethnic groups. The following points may be of interest to the reader:

1. Even at this stage, quite a number of Vietnamese still bear grudge against the American government for having abandoned the Nationalist Vietnamese to their lamentable fate by curtailing all forms of aids at the crucial moment when the communists were preparing to launch their general offensive on the remaining territory of Free Vietnam. Though in later years it became quite obvious that the U.S. Government was acting in the interests of the American people, yet their policy was taken for a sell-out to the enemy. A period of ten years has gone by. It is hoped that time could have brought solace and comfort to the Nationalist Vietnamese. The main query now remains: Is the U.S. Government going to do anything for the hundreds of thousands of former servicemen of the Republic of Vietnam currently suffering in communist so-called "re-education camps"?

2. Corruption under the Thieu regime played a significant role in shattering the Nationalist cause. Today, in spite of the ten years that have passed, hundreds of thousands of conscientious Vietnamese patriots still put the blame on Thieu and his lackeys for the loss of the nation to those barbarous Soviet henchmen. Currently, a number of former corrupt

officials of the defunct regime are still politically ambitious by actively scheming to return to power. They could be daydreaming, but ambition has no boundary.

3. While settling in free countries, the majority of overseas Vietnamese are exerting special efforts to preserve their 5000-year-old culture and to remind their descendants of their traditional national roots. However, some others now enjoy materialistic pleasures so much that they would wish to forget all about their origin and would prefer to be Americanized the sooner the better. Such feeble-minded attitude is one of the causes of dissension and division in most Vietnamese communities today. The annoying issue is that those deracinated elements are raking money, through their professions and trades, from their Vietnamese countrymen in this country, yet they quietly depart from the Vietnamese mainstream. It sounds queer and contradictory, but it is part of the sad reality.

4. Other groups advocate that being overseas, they should forget the past entirely even if that past was good and benevolent. They nurture the wrong concept by reasoning that "the U.S. is a different world. This is no longer Vietnam. They want to forget Vietnam forever and adopt the new American way of life. Keep Vietnam in oblivion. These setbacks will be common among those disillusioned elements. Remarkable social change in the livelihood of the newcomers is in the offing. The first decade has indeed been a period of challenge and trial among the Vietnamese expatriates whose hearts and souls have been so much disrupted due to despair, sufferings and frustrations.

The preceding paragraphs have presented a rather gloomy picture of the Vietnamese newcomers in the United States. But not all is negative about these new arrivals. There is also the brighter side of the picture thanks to the courage and patience of these hardworking and intelligent people. In reality, the candidate wishes to present firstly the negative aspects of the Vietnamese immigrants in this country before having words of praise for them.

Compared with other ethnic groups who have come to resettle in the United States, such as the Irish, Chinese, Japanese, Koreans, Philipinos, Mexicans,... The Vietnamese are considered relatively more successful in the various walks of life in a record time. This is due to their patience, dilligence, and above all to their adaptability to new circumstances. Several Vietnamese were not professionals in any particular trades, since a great number had to serve in the armed forces nearly all their lives because of the prolonged war. But when they came to this country, they willingly and earnestly learned new skills and became capable technicians and specialists. Most of them had the problem of language barrier, but after only one or two years they became conversant fluently in English with local people. As for school children and college students, it took them only a couple of months to be familiarized with the new school atmosphere and in only a couple of years, they had caught up with their American classmates without too much hardship.

The main reasons for these successes were due to the fact that among the contingents of refugees who came here in Spring, 1975, a rather high percentage had quite solid educational background: professionals, artists, intellectuals, high-ranking military officers... who could adapt themselves to new living conditions without serious transitional problems.

Whereas most other ethnic immigrants came to this country previously mainly for "economic" reasons.

In terms of business enterprises, even if the Vietnamese newcomers had to confront great odds against them, such as: language barrier, lack of capital, poor knowledge of modern business practices and redtapes, unfamiliar environment, no business connections... which at first seemed to be unsurmountable obstacles, they would resignedly learn all the details to apply to their trades and businesses. Most of them work hard, earn their living honestly and decently with the exception of some crooked elements that exist not only in the Vietnamese communities but also in any other ethnic communities.

As a new arrival in this country ten years ago, the author came across some "old-hand" Vietnamese families, who had settled in the United States prior to the events of 1975. They would speak English to their children to the despair of the newcomers, who could not but think that just a short sojourn in this country and Vietnamese children were going to forget their mother-tongue altogether. What a dramatic blow to the 50-century-old Vietnamese culture! What a shame to lose one's national identity after only such a short lapse of time, while it is observed that the Jewish people have succeeded in preserving their traditional culture in spite of nearly two thousand years of living in exile in all corners of the world, and while the black people are in search of their roots!

But ten years have gone by, Vietnamese high-school and college students have shown signs of proudly reserving special consideration for their national culture while adopting American culture. These youngsters and youths still show great pride in using the Vietnamese language among themselves as witnessed through countless school magazines in Vietnamese published recently. Cultural performances have also been staged in numerous college auditoriums and theaters in an all-out effort to promote Vietnamese culture among the residents in the various Vietnamese communities throughout the United States. Furthermore, thanks to modern electronic devices and appliances, especially through the audio and video tapes, Vietnamese literature and music are having a greater and greater audience among the expatriates.

On the other hand, serious publishers are also contributing special efforts in effectively preserving the national culture among the Vietnamese currently residing in the United States and other free countries. Valuable literary works have been reprinted in sufficient numbers to respond to the steady demands of the Vietnamese readers, while new works are also being written and published, and new musical hits composed. All these exceptional efforts are contributing directly to the preservation and popularization of Vietnamese culture in foreign lands, while the communist regime has been burning and destroying thousands of valuable literary and philosophical works - the greatest treasures of a nation.

It was pessimistically thought that the Vietnamese younger generations overseas would be culturally degenerated or deracinated, but quite to the contrary, it is now obvious that most of them still possess the Vietnamese Soul in them, and thanks to this phenomenon, the Vietnamese culture will survive as long as the Vietnamese race exists everywhere in the Free World. It seems that Vietnamese parents are too preoccupied with working hard for a living and to support normally large households. The inevitable result is that they have no time to talk to their children about cultural matters. Nevertheless, Vietnamese culture seems to be penetrating into almost every Vietnamese family through various media: the printed books, newspapers, magazines, radio messages, audio cassettes and especially Vietnamese-language video tapes now readily available at the numerous video stores.

Other than the aforesaid media, currently hundreds of Vietnamese college students volunteer their time to serve as Vietnamese-language instructors to kids in most Vietnamese communities. Fortunately the Vietnamese were the first Asians to have adopted the Roman alphabet to their writing for nearly 200 years. This is the main reason for the high literacy rate among the Vietnamese. Consequently, the preservation and propagation of Vietnamese culture overseas could be carried out with more effect than some other cultures.

The Vietnamese are commemorating their tenth anniversary in this free country, and undoubtedly many a family will recollect all the events and happenings during the first decade to serve as a general review of past experiences so as to make better plans for a brighter future in the coming decade. It will be another challenging stage for the pioneers' continuing efforts and relentless courage.

94

TABLE

Monthly Household Income of $800 or More and Individual Weekly Wages
of $200 or More for Different Groups of OSI-Surveyed Refugees, 1975-1980

| SURVEYED POPULATION | WAVE | WHEN CONDUCTED | PERCENT WITH MONTHLY HOUSE-HOLD INCOME OF $800 OR MORE | PERCENT WITH WEEKLY EARNINGS OF OF $200 OR MORE |
|---|---|---|---|---|
| Vietnamese | I | Summer 1975 | 14.9% | n/a |
| " | II | Nov-Dec 1975 | 32.4 | 3.2 |
| " | III | July-Aug 1976 | 41.2 | 5.3 |
| " | IV | Nov-Dec 1976 | 43.8 | n/a |
| " | V | July-Aug 1977 | 51.4 | 14.3 |
| " | VI | Nov-Dec 1978 | 70.0 | 33.7 |
| " | VII | Apr-June 1979 | 75.6 | n/a |
| " | VIII | Oct-Nov 1979 | 79.4 | 49.9 |
| " | IX | Oct-Nov 1980 | 67.6 | 53.7 |
| Cambodian | VI | Nov-Dec 1978 | 63.1 | 29.7 |
| " | VII | Apr-June 1979 | 74.5 | 38.2 |
| " | VIII | Oct-Nov 1979 | 73.8 | 40.7 |
| " | IX | Oct-Nov 1980 | 64.5 | 38.8 |
| Laotian | VII | Apr-June 1979 | 67.4 | 27.9 |
| " | VIII | Oct-Nov 1979 | 59.7 | 36.9 |
| " | IX | Oct-Nov 1980 | 55.8 | 37.1 |

Source: OSI Reports (Generally Tables 13 for earnings, and Tables 15 for income).

TABLE

Average Weekly Wages for Five Groups of Indochinese Refugees and for US Production or Nonsupervisory Workers, 1981, 1982 and 1983

(in US dollars unless otherwise noted)

| | US DATA | | INDOCHINESE DATA | | | | |
|---|---|---|---|---|---|---|---|
| PERIOD | Unemployment Rate for Year | Production or Nonsupervisory Workers | Vietnamese | Lao | Ethnic Chinese | Cambodian | Hmong |
| October 1981 | 7.6% | 260.44 | 356.61 | 179.66 | 246.08 | 341.14 | 218.26 |
| October 1982 | 9.7 | 270.31 | 235.08 | 176.10 | 173.28 | 170.60 | 183.84 |
| October 1983 | 9.6 | 287.70p | 219.23 | 181.03 | 182.36 | 170.56 | 201.38 |

Sources: Unemployment rate, 1981, Statistical Abstract of the U.S. 1982-83, Table 656; comparable data for subsequent years secured by telephone with the Bureau of Labor Statistics. Earnings data for production or nonsupervisory workers from Employment and Earnings, January issues, 1982, 1983 and 1984, Table C-1. Earnings data for Indochinese workers from OSI Surveys, Waves X, XI, and XII (unpublished ORR statistics).

Note: Samples of the Cambodian and Hmong workers are relatively small and should be used with caution. All data are for those who are employed.

The letter "p" indicates preliminary data.

Transition Program for Refugee Children
FY 1983

## By Indochinese & Other

|  | Number | Percent |
|---|---|---|
| Indochinese refugee children | 93,877 | 83% |
| Other refugee children | 18,911 | 17% |
| Total | 112,788 | 100% |

## By Levels

|  | Number | Percent |
|---|---|---|
| Number of refugee children in elementary schools | 51,156 | 45% |
| Number of refugee children in secondary schools | 61,632 | 55% |
|  | 112,788 | 100% |

## By Indochinese & Other and levels

|  | Elementary | Secondary | Total |
|---|---|---|---|
| Indochinese refugee children | 41,116 | 52,761 | 93,877 |
| Other refugee children | 10,040 | 8,871 | 18,911 |

Refugees have a labor force participation rate higher than the United States population, but also an unemployment rate that, at 15 percent, is well above the national average. Concurrently there is an increase in English language competence. Of those refugees in the country over 3 years, only 6 percent appear to speak no English, and nearly two-thirds report the ability to speak English well or fluently. Enrollment in English language training drops over time, as does the receipt of cash assistance. One variable that does not exhibit such a trend is enrollment in other training or educational programs. Southeast Asian refugees continue to seek training and education throughout their residence in the U.S. Indeed, the data suggest that education and training may increase over time as refugees gain competence in English and more frequently and successfully participate in the labor force.

Increasing economic self-sufficiency is one part of this overall process of adjustment to the United States. But the achievement of economic self-sufficiency is more complicated. An examination of the differences between refugee households who are receiving cash assistance and those not receiving cash assistance highlights the difficulties faced in becoming economically self-sufficient. Two factors deserve particular note: First, cash assistance

## Background Characteristics by Year of Entry

| Year of Entry | Average Years of Education | Percent Speaking No English | Percent Speaking English Well or Fluently |
|---|---|---|---|
| 1982 | 6.8 | 42.3% | 17.4% |
| 1981 | 7.0 | 52.3% | 8.4% |
| 1980 | 6.8 | 57.1% | 6.0% |
| 1979 | 7.6 | 41.9% | 19.0% |
| 1978 | 8.2 | 53.7% | 9.0% |
| 1976-7 | 7.1 | 31.8% | 26.8% |
| 1975 | 9.5 | 30.6% | 25.2% |

Note: These figures refer to characteristics of incoming refugees at time of arrival in the United States and should not be confused with the *current* characteristics of these refugees

recipient households are notably larger than non-recipient households. They include a greater proportion of dependent children and thus are likely to have higher demands on the fewer adult wage earners in the family.

## Patterns in Refugee Adjustment

| | Length of Residence in U.S. (in months) | | | | | | |
|---|---|---|---|---|---|---|---|
| | 0-6 | 7-12 | 13-18 | 19-24 | 25-30 | 31-36 | over 36 |
| Labor force participation | 21.6% | 33.3% | 36.6% | 54.6% | 48.9% | 59.0% | 68.4% |
| Unemployment | 75.0% | 49.7% | 40.8% | 41.0% | 29.3% | 26.4% | 14.8% |
| Weekly income of employed persons | $150.10 | $156.43 | $153.92 | $180.66 | $157.74 | $181.71 | $236.32 |
| Percent in English training | 58.5% | 47.4% | 54.5% | 39.7% | 30.0% | 25.6% | 11.5% |
| Percent in other training or schooling | 23.4% | 27.4% | 26.4% | 27.1% | 35.9% | 30.1% | 31.6% |
| Percent speaking no English* | 26.9% | 25.3% | 18.6% | 15.1% | 13.5% | 9.2% | 6.2% |
| Percent speaking English well* | 18.5% | 15.1% | 23.1% | 24.5% | 35.0% | 41.4% | 65.9% |
| Percent receiving cash assistance* | 82.7% | 81.7% | 75.6% | 67.3% | 54.0% | 46.3% | 22.7% |

Note: All except the asterisked figures refer to the population aged 16 and over. The asterisked figures refer to the entire population regardless of age. Specifically, the cash assistance figure is the percentage of the entire sampled population residing in households receiving such assistance.

## EFFECTS OF ENGLISH LANGUAGE PROFICIENCY

| Ability to Speak and Understand English | Labor Force Participation | Unemployment | Average Weekly Wages |
|---|---|---|---|
| Not at all | 25.2% | 36.1% | $168.29 |
| A little | 55.5% | 23.4% | $179.26 |
| Well | 61.8% | 13.8% | $208.45 |
| Fluently | 63.2% | 12.8% | $246.46 |

### Achieving Economic Self-Sufficiency

The achievement of economic self-sufficiency hinges on the mixtures of refugee skills, refugee needs, and the resources available in the communities in which refugees resettle. The occupational and educational skills that refugees bring with them to the United States influence their prospects for self-sufficiency. Data from the 1983 survey indicate two modest changes in the characteristics of arriving Southeast Asian refugees since 1975: First, there is a clear drop in educational level between 1975 and later arrivals, but relative similarity in prior education among all those arriving since 1975. 1975 arrivals had received, on the average, 9.5 years of formal education. For those arriving since 1975, the average number of years of education has remained about 7.5. Second, there appears to be less English language competence at arrival among those entering the U.S. since 1977 than among those entering during 1975-1977. However, this pattern is broken by the apparently higher English skills of 1982 and particularly 1983 arrivals. This increased English language skill may reflect the provision of ESL training in refugee processing centers overseas.

## BACKGROUND CHARACTERISTICS BY YEAR OF ENTRY

| Year of Entry | Average Years of Education | % Speaking No English | % Speaking English well or Fluently |
|---|---|---|---|
| 1983 | 7.7 | 29.4% | 12.2% |
| 1982 | 7.5 | 29.9% | 8.5% |
| 1981 | 6.8 | 36.8% | 7.1% |
| 1980 | 7.4 | 37.7% | 9.7% |
| 1979 | 7.9 | 37.1% | 7.2% |
| 1978 | 7.5 | 35.1% | 5.5% |
| 1976-7 | 7.6 | 25.1% | 23.1% |
| 1975 | 9.4 | 30.4% | 32.1% |

Note: These figures refer to characteristics of incoming refugees at time of arrival in the United States and should not be confused with the *current* characteristics of thse refugees.

## Patterns in the Adjustment of
## Southeast Asian Refugees

### Length of Residence in Months

|  | 0-6 | 7-12 | 13-18 | 19-24 | 25-30 | 31-36 | over 36 |
|---|---|---|---|---|---|---|---|
| Labor force participation | 12.0% | 33.9% | 42.5% | 38.0% | 45.4% | 52.5% | 63.9% |
| Unemployment | 83.6% | 47.5% | 28.4% | 29.8% | 18.1% | 17.7% | 15.5% |
| Weekly income of employed persons | 151.50 | 116.88 | 153.77 | 134.49 | 163.50 | 166.10 | 223.70 |
| Percent in English training | 57.9% | 53.1% | 35.6% | 38.5% | 32.6% | 35.9% | 14.6% |
| Percent in other training or schooling | 23.7% | 15.9% | 33.7% | 35.0% | 24.0% | 31.7% | 30.4% |
| Percent speaking English well or fluently* | 27.6% | 18.4% | 37.9% | 38.7% | 30.1% | 38.9% | 62.8% |
| Percent speaking no English* | 18.8% | 20.4% | 13.3% | 12.4% | 21.2% | 19.9% | 8.5% |
| Percent in households receiving cash assistance* | 77.0% | 81.3% | 64.0% | 61.6% | 67.7% | 49.4% | 32.0% |

Note: All except the asterisked figures refer to the population aged sixteen and over. The asterisked figures refer to the entire population.

REFUGEE SELF-SUFFICIENCY INCREASES OVER TIME
Percent of CWS Refugee Cases Who Were Self-sufficient as of the Fall of 1983

Source: Making It On Their Own: From Refugee Sponsorship
to Self-sufficiency; A Survey on Refugee Resettlement
and Adjustment by Church World Service, January, 1984.

Chapter 3

## SYNOPSIS

- Case Studies.
- The Ten Representative Entrepreneurial Activities.

    1.- The Vietnamese Confectionery Store.
    2.- Home Painting.
    3.- Egg-Roll Manufacturing.
    4.- Land Development and Home Building.
    5.- The Medical Professions.
    6.- The Rice Noodle Soup Shop.
    7.- The Convenience Store Business.
    8.- The Publishing Business.
    9.- The Technicians and Assemblers.
    10.- The Oriental Food Business.

# CHAPTER 3

## SYNOPSIS

After ten years of exceptionally dilligent work and extreme efforts, the Vietnamese newcomers to this country have set an exemplary model of the immigrant's image to their American contemporary hosts.

In the wake of the fall of Saigon into communists' hands in Spring, 1975, with the termination of a relatively free democracy in that part of the world, great numbers of Vietnamese resettled in the U.S.A. and many became entrepreneurs, who can be categorized as follows:

TRADITIONAL SKILLS: Those who would carry on their traditional trades brought over from their native land.

IMPROVED TRADITIONAL SKILLS: Those who would improve their former skills by taking advantage of modern U.S. facilities.

NEW SKILLS: Those who have learned new trades and skills since their resettlement in the U.S.A.

Before proceeding any further, the reader is asked to refer to the table of trades and skills (p. 106) in order to have a general view of the various trades and professions that are being practiced by these new arrivals in the U.S. today:

Three main groups:
a.- Traditional skills (brought over from Vietnam).
b.- Updated traditional skills.
c.- New skills acquired while taking refuge.

## A.- TRADITIONAL:

- Bakery, confectionery, Vietnamese grocery stores
- Doll-making
- Dressmaking
- Drug stores, pharmacies
- Educational services: Language schools, Translations, Art Schools.
- Embroidery
- Entertainment: Dance halls, cabarets
- Fabric Shops
- Food manufacturing: Fish sauce, shrimp paste, meat pie...
- Fortune telling: Occult sciences
- Gift shops
- Jewelry stores
- Medical: Oriental medicine, Acupuncture, Herbal medications
- Movie-houses
- Religious orders
- Restaurants: Rice noodle soups, seven-course beefs...
- Pawn shops
- Shoe stores
- Vegetable growing
- Wood carving
- Writers: Novels, poems, newspapers, magazines...

## B.- IMPROVED TRADITIONAL:

- Air-conditioners: Sales, repairs...
- Architecture
- Auto-driving school
- Auto parts stores
- Banking, savings & loan
- Bartending

- Bookstores
- Building contractors
- Butcher shops
- Electronic, TV stores
- Electronic servicing
- Engineering
- Entertainment: musical bands, cassettes
- Fishing and Shrimping
- Flower shops
- Food manufacturing: Egg-rolls, pork pie, beef loaf, shrimp
  sauce, shrimp paste, anchovy sauce...
- Furniture
- Graphic arts & designs
- Grocery stores
- Import - Export
- Insect Extermination
- Journalism
- Landscaping
- Law practice
- Martial arts instruction
- Medical: Western-style clinics, physicians, dentists,
  surgeons...
- Painting
- Photography 1-hour lab
- Print shops
- Publishing
- Restaurant: Gourmet store
- Security installations: Burglar bars
- Supermarkets
- Teaching
- Technical schools
- Travel agencies
- White collar jobs: Tellers, bookkeepers, clerks, secretaries...

## C.- NEW SKILLS

- Accounting: Advanced American systems.
- Apartment ownership and management.
- Automobile dealerships: new & used
- Auto sales
- Blue collar jobs: Factory hands, mechanics, assemblers, welders
- Bookstores: adult
- Brokerage firms: insurance, real estate, financial services
- Car washing
- Car towing service
- Copying (quick) stores
- Convenience stores
- Computer stores: hardware, software
- Daycare centers
- Food manufacturing
- Freight services
- Game rooms: Video, pool, billiards
- Hair styling
- Home building
- Investment services
- Janitorial services
- License & permit service
- Liquor stores
- Marketing consultation
- Office equipment sales
- Plumbing
- Private detective agencies
- Tabloid publications
- Tax return service
- Video: Sales, services, rental, dubbing
- Washateria
- Word processing

## SUCCESSES:

### A.- TRADITIONAL TRADES:

- Jewelry stores
- Medical: Oriental medicinal herbalists
- Restaurant: Rice noodle soup (phở)
- Vegetables: Growing & nursery

### B.- UPDATED TRADES:

- Fishery and shrimping
- Food manufacturing: egg-roll making
- Food manufacturing: meat-pie making (giò, chả)
- Medical: Western-style physicians, surgeons, dentists, pharmacists

### C.- NEW TRADES:

- Stores: Cultural books, cassettes, videos, art pieces, musical instruments...
- Hair-styling
- Liquor stores
- Washaterias

## FAILURES:

### A.- TRADITIONAL TRADES

- Entertainment: Dance halls, cabarets
- Restaurants: General
- Shoe stores
- Writing: Novels, poems...

## B.- UPDATED TRADES:

- Banking, savings & loans...
- Graphic arts & design
- Import & export
- Law practice

## C.- NEW TRADES

- Convenience stores
- Game rooms: Video, pool, billiards
- Home building
- Investments: Stocks, bonds, real estate, commodities

The above brief list was based on a general survey to work out the average success and failure cases. There are, of course, exceptions as in any line of business. Please read the case studies, pp. 113 to 200, in order to draw an overall conclusion on the business activities advocated by the Vietnamese resettlers in the U.S. since 1975.

## CASE STUDIES

The author has spent the past seven years following closely the progress and evolution of the Vietnamese business world as observed in some major and minor communities set up by the resettlers in the U.S.A. The author thinks it would be appropriate to present to the reader the accounts of his documentation in a restrictive and representative manner by describing ten typical cases in a way that could enable the reader to have an overall picture of the Vietnamese business circles as evolved in this country during the past decade.

The reader will deduce from the case presentations in order

to realize the enormous efforts contributed and the great shortcomings borne by the Vietnamese expatriates when doing business in the new land. Both successes and failures in the diversified but typical entrepreneurial ventures will be depicted in this study.

It is hoped that by stating and exposing the problems being faced by the resettlers, adequate solutions could be worked out for the benefit of those who care to learn from the studies, investigations, observations, personal experiences, expensive mistakes... patiently and systematically noted and recorded by the candidate whose ambition and desire are to serve his fellow-people through his humble contribution for the betterment of the business circles among the various Vietnamese communities spread out widely over this immense land.

As there is currently too little documentation on the economic and financial aspects concerning the Vietnamese ethnic minority in the U.S.A. available in any libraries including the major ones such as the Library of Congress, Harvard University, Cornell University and Yale University, the candidate deems it best to tackle the problem with case studies rather than by any other procedures.

The typical pattern used for accounting for each case is based on the following main points:

a.- Description of the business
b.- Performance
c.- Management
d.- Policies and decisions
e.- Ethics
f.- Personnel
g.- Objectives
h.- Planning
i.- Inventory
j.- Organization
k.- Actuating function
l.- Evaluative function
m.- Concluding thought
n.- Estimating balance sheet

The cases were actually under study and observation by the author. As stated earlier in this chapter, some entrepreneurs failed and went out of business, others were successful and showed good prospects for a brighter future. All the statements concerning the "cases" were based on exact, experienced facts. The author's position, as far as this section of the paper is concerned, only offers his personal opinion at the conclusive parts of each typical case. He would carefully record the experiences, ideas and prejudices of those who were involved in their respective "cases." Recommendations and suggestions, however, will be offered in a separate chapter.

All the entrepreneurs who were the subjects in particular "cases" would want to maintain their anonymity. With due respect to their desire, the candidate finds himself fully obligated to comply to that rule of ethics (Note: Thus the names are fictitious while the personalities are real). Those who failed in their business undertakings should make a point to learn more conscientiously either through the hard way, that is, the bitter experience, or through the numerous academic and professional courses being offered at various continuing education institutions and colleges. Those who succeeded in their entrepreneurial endeavors are rewarded not only financially, but very often they seem to stress the emotional, spiritual and righteous satisfaction of their enterprises.

At the end of each case, the candidate would add some personal remarks which, hopefully, might contribute to the improvement of a particular line of business.

## 1.- The Vietnamese Confectionery Store.

Although the U.S.A. is reputed for manufacturing and marketing the greatest variety of confectionery including candies, chocolates, chewing gums, cookies... The Vietnamese newcomers have a particular preference for some types of Vietnamese confectionery. Due to their customs and homesickness, they missed their favorite items for only the first couple of months. By 1976 - the year of the cat - a few sorts of Vietnamese confectionery were already put on sale in some Oriental food stores on Chartre Street, Houston, as well as in other oriental stores in areas where there were sizeable Vietnamese and Chinese communities. Those items included sweet rice puddings (bánh chưng), sweetened preserved lotus seeds (mứt sen), sweet rice seedling cakes (bánh cốm), pork pie (giò lụa) and so forth.

Those varieties were snatched up like hot cakes by the local Vietnamese residents, and instantly the enterprising newcomers were aware of a ready market for their products. Among them was the family of Binh who used to own a confectionery store on Gia Long Street in Saigon prior to the exodus. After some investigative time spent in locating the supply sources of the main ingredients and altering some food processors and appliances, available in local stores such as Sears, Montgomery Ward, Foley's... he started his Vietnamese confectionery factory in his home and began marketing his products through the oriental food stores - his main outlets at that time.

Business was booming right away, for the operation was so simple. Since the market was already there, all Binh had to do was to put his professional and traditional knowledge into the production of his goods. His case is a typical example of transferring a traditional trade from Saigon to Houston with little changes or improvements whatsoever. Production of some "native" food items belongs to this category.

Binh's clientele consisted chiefly of Vietnamese who would purchase their "national" confectionery at normal times, but on special occasions, he would find customers flocking to his "home factory" in greater numbers:

A. The lunar year has at least four major festivals when Vietnamese would buy candies, preserved fruits and cakes for gifts to relatives and friends, or for offerings to their ancestors:

- the lunar new year (which falls in late January, or early February)
- the Fifth Moon Festival
- the Mid-Autumn Festival
- and Christmas!

B. The engagement ceremony: The bride's family usually requests that the groom's family contribute, as in homage, a certain number of "gift packages", each of which may contain: two rice-seedling cakes (bánh cốm), two tins of fragrant tea, and some betel nuts. Each of such package may cost in the neighborhood of $20 to $30. So if the bride's family has quite a few friends, it may "demand" for 200 gift packages and this would mean an initial expense of around $4,000 to $6,000. Quite a sum! It is customary to accompany the gift package with the announcement cards which are hand-carried courteously and ceremoniously to each acquaintance's home.

This preliminary stage is subsequently followed by the wedding party where a few hundred relatives and friends are invited to a sumptuous dinner, ·and of course, again, Vietnamese cakes and preserved fruits are served. That's how our confectioner friend makes his new fortune. Marriages among the Vietnamese in the U.S. are at a more frequent pace in spite of the great expenses. Probably thanks to the financing system available in this country: Marry now, pay later.

Since 1980, Vietnamese confectionery "home factories" and retail stores have been opened in most major cities where there are Vietnamese communities. Houston (Texas) has at least three outfits, New Orleans (Louisiana) two, Orange County (California) five, Seattle (Washington) two... They simply turn out their products in the traditional manner; still the same ingredients, same simple packaging, mostly done by hand. It should be about time for this line of business to be modernized as the Japanese and Korean residents have done so. It will not be long before competition will compel the current Vietnamese confectioners to adapt modern techniques for organization, management, production and marketing.

The greatest oversight in Binh's business was that he was completely ignorant of the prevailing laws and regulations governing the production of cooked and ready-to-eat foodstuffs. He was producing them illegally all that time. He did not even put labels on his products, and so anyone could imitate and counterfeit his goods. In reality he was not trying to break any laws, but the main shortcoming was that he did not know much about the existing laws and regulations in the U.S.

This is a typical case among quite a number of Vietnamese newcomers in this country. The author has heard of incidents where similar food-producers were snatched red-handed by law-enforcement officers and eventually prosecuted by the authorities. Also among these pitiful law-breakers were producers of egg-rolls, meat pies, shrimp paste, fish sauce, candies, cakes, cookies, preserved fruits. Agencies that are in charge of assisting refugees should take this type of business activity into consideration and offer sound legal advice to those who may be infringing upon the laws unknowingly.

Binh was typical of the group of business people who worked hard for their living in conformity with truly traditional Vietnamese style. Likewise is the case of An as described in the following case. Binh is complacent with his business as long as it can afford him the income to provide for his family. He would think that sophisticated management know-how would be unnecessary for his modest and homely undertaking. Candidly he would never see the necessity of this fuss about modern business techniques. But in order to survive in business, even in a very small business such as the one that Binh was doing in this country, he needed to be educated professionally so that he might conform himself to local laws and regulations. Furthermore, should other competitors come into the market with modern business knowledge, they could eliminate Binh from the scene without difficulty.

The author observes here that some publications in the Vietnamese language are needed to inform these business-people in order to help them survive in this entirely new environment. Thus, in a way, we find that some Vietnamese small business people think they are currently "successful", but in years to come will they be able to survive under more pressing circumstances? Binh's case could be placed in the "success-failure" category, since his business is having so many shortcomings as far as U.S. criteria are concerned. If business people like him do not take the trouble in improving their trades by acquiring useful business and legal information they will inevitably lose ground to those who are more knowledgeable.

## 2. HOME PAINTING

An was a non-commissioned officer (NCO) in the navy of the former Republic of Vietnam before he took flight with his shipmates on the eve of the fall of Saigon into communists' hands in late April 1975. In his capacity as a non-commissioned naval officer in Vietnam, one of his customary jobs was the charge of a group of sailors whose duty was to keep their vessel (a destroyer) clean and properly painted.

After Saigon, he was placed in a refugee camp at Fort Chaffee, Arkansas. In August 1975, he came to Houston, Texas, where he was sponsored by an American family. Being an independent young man, 22 years of age and unmarried with no children, he did not need or want to be on any form of welfare assistance. He only wanted to work. His sponsor suggested that he work as a helper to a professional home painter in the neighborhood. An jumped at the idea, for the job suited him perfectly, even though he was handicapped by the language barrier and lack of business knowledge in the new land.

After a year working under the tutorship of his painter boss, An learned quite a few notions of the trade and enjoyed the full-time job which was bringing him a reasonably good income and many fringe benefits; outdoor work on various locations. full working time yet with sufficient leisure during which he picked up his English lessons, and plenty of opportunity to meet new and interesting people.

As An acquired additional knowledge of home painting, his American boss and friend - a truly generous Christian - encouraged him to start his own business. An duly followed the good advice and was soon on his own in another area in the south-eastern section of Houston.

By word of mouth, one satisfied customer told another and this system worked for him as soon as he had got the first assignment in the neighborhood. An was also intelligent enough to use as many free sources of publicity as possible, such as: the community bulletin boards in supermarkets, drugstores, washaterias... His hand-printed bulletin board notices and a few hundred quick-printed fliers handed out in the subdivisions was a good approach as people seemed to think that the refugee needed work badly, therefore would charge below the normal going rate.

An also learned from his former boss how to work out free estimates for prospective customers, who all wanted to make sure they would not be taken advantage of. He also made use of the local tabloid and regional "green sheet" for his initial ad campaign, and this was not at all expensive: only five dollars for a three-line ad in the classified section.

As business flourished, An engaged two Vietnamese youngsters to help him. There was not much management work as it was only a sort of family business, so he had not much concern over matters such as policy planning and decision making. His business expanded mostly through the good publicity generated from the fine job he rendered to the satisfied customers in his subdivision.

The local paint store-owner, who carried a good reliable line, had a fondness and respect for the young foreign newcomer. An tried to build up his credibility with all those he dealt with and in only two years he won the confidence of all. An's new acquaintances, needless to say, helped him most effectively in bringing him additional jobs, and eventually his home painting business landed him with subcontracts to handle tens of homes at a time from major contractors and regional home builders. The years 1978-1980 were his most prosperous period, when he had to expand his crews to over twenty members, but 1981 through 1984 the home-building industry in Houston was clobbered by recession. Currently, in spite of the unfavorable economic situation in Houston, An is still having enough contracts to handle with his crews of painters by offering to repaint used homes "for a good job at a reasonable price."

An made it his policy to ask his customers to select and buy their own paints and he always suggested to them to buy first-grade, high-quality products. Good paint could make a painter look good, so he would never cut corners here. But if the customer asked him to secure the paint he would naturally select the best. As a result, inventory is never a problem for this small-scale business owner; in fact, his inventory is available at his favorite paint store-owner's warehouse!

Regarding starting capital in this business, An did not have to face any major problems as the check-list for materials includes inexpensive items: brushes, spirits of oleum (for cleaning and thinning), ladders, dropcloths, scrapers, rags, used nylon stockings, simple tools (hammers, nails, adjustable wrenches...), wire, old newspaper, a small box (wooden or milk container), safety glasses, painting clothes and shoes.

An always wanted his customers to be fully satisfied with his work. Every one of his customers should have the feeling that he (the customer) got a $1000 paint job for $500. Nothing ruined a job like spots on shingles, driveways, mailboxes, and porchlights. A little effort and a discreet use of dropcloths would keep the surrounding vegetations and other uncoated areas in their original condition.

An did not have to acquire sophisticated knowledge in business administration in order to run his modest operation successfully. If he is satisfied with his current income, he should carry on the business diligently and honestly in the years to come and should certainly enjoy an average standard of living. However, if he is more ambitious and would like to expand his business on a larger scale, he has to improve on several other aspects of modern business administration that will be discussed in a subsequent chapter.

Currently, in the numerous Vietnamese communities all over the states, small-sized home painting units run by the new settlers are very common. This line of business can bring them reasonably comfortable incomes while no special technology or English language fluency is required. These families have a feeling that they are being self-employed and are not bothered too much with the "lay off" problem as witnessed during the recessionary years of 1981 and 1982. However, so far nearly all of these businesses are limited to a sort of family-style enterprise. Not a single group has developed into any large modernly-organized corporation. This could be due to lack of capital and sophisticated business organization.

Table    Growth in Number of Economic Development Projects and Enterprises, 1979-1983

| Year | Sewing | Farming | Grocery Stores | Other Enterprises | Total |
|------|--------|---------|----------------|-------------------|-------|
| 1979 | 2      | --      | --             | --                | 2     |
| 1980 | 8      | --      | 1              | 1                 | 10    |
| 1981 | 14     | --      | 12             | 3                 | 29    |
| 1982 | 23     | 9       | 27             | 9                 | 68    |
| 1983 | 28     | 11      | 28             | 11                | 78    |

(Promotion of Self-Sufficiency Programs among the Hmong, an ethnic tribal group of Vietnam, in the U.S.A.)

Source: Refugee Resettlement Office.

## 3. EGG ROLL MANUFACTURING

The subject in this case study, fictitiously named Can, was an undergraduate student who came to the U.S. to further his college education with the help of a Colombo Plan scholarship in 1972. In April 1975 when the Republic of Vietnam was overrun by the communists, communication with his family in Saigon was severed and Can was left alone in this country without relatives except for a couple of classmates.

He was quick to realize that Vietnamese and other Asians would be coming to this country in great numbers due to the exodus. Can thought of providing a very well-known and simple food - the egg roll - already introduced earlier by the Chinese immigrants in the later part of the 19th century in the San Francisco area - an item to be found in most Americanized Chinese restaurants all over the fifty states.

However, the Vietnamese have their own kind of egg-roll, called "chả giò", which is considered by most connoisseurs and gourmets as more delicious and sophisticated than the Chinese egg roll since its recipe contains ingredients of higher quality such as: dried mushrooms, dehydrated wood fungus (mục nhĩ), crabmeat. lean pork, vermicelli, egg yoke - all rolled in rice paper (bánh tráng). The rolls are then deep-fried. When dipped in a dilute spicy fish sauce and eaten with raw lettuce and other mints, it tastes superb! But on a commercial basis, the cost of turning out such a product en masse would not be feasible for marketing*.

Can, in spite of his preference for the Vietnamese "chả giò", had to adopt the Chinese egg-roll recipe for several practical reasons: the ingredients (cabbage leaves, pork, carrot, bean sprout, green onion leaves) are much cheaper and look more

---

*Appendix B, p. **240**

colorful; the thick wheat wrapper is always available through local Chinese noodle producers, and when deep-fried, the wheat wrapper becomes crispy and could be kept so under infra-red light or warmed up in microwave oven very handily and speedily.

Too often the businessman makes his decisions on whim or after a superficial appraisal. He can usually survive such decisions when they involve the purchase of, say, a car. He cannot, however, adopt a casual attitude about buying or starting up a business. He must have the patience to learn all there is to know about a particular business before he invests his time, energy, and financial resources in it.[1]  Can has learned through the failure of some friends and in this case he has weighed the pros and cons quite carefully.

The decision was made and Can plunged into the business by taking over a nearly run-down but ongoing taco shop which he paid just $3,000 cash for the entire operation including a tiny retail store, storage space, and a food-preparing area totalling less than 900 square feet. (That store had already changed hands at least four times because of poor organization.)

Can did not have any previous experience in the food manufacturing field, but he was more fortunate than most other Vietnamese newcomers who came to the U.S. almost empty-handed. Can had some capital and could speak English better than most of his Vietnamese counterparts. He was possessed with a strong belief that Orientals as well as Americans would like his egg-rolls as long as his product was tasty and priced reasonably. So he concentrated all his efforts, physical and mental, toward making and improving on that unique food item — the egg-roll, which is nourishing, low in calories, priced competitively and, above all, it tastes good.

---

[1]*Bernard Greissman, editor, "How To Run a Small Business," 5th ed. by J.K. Lasser Tax Institute, McGraw-Hill Book Co., New York, 1983, p. 1.*

In the beginning none of the people in his outfit (five in all) had any knowledge of large volume egg-roll production techniques. They carried out all the production stages manually with some sort of logical labor-distribution system. As time passed and sales increased, he recruited more helpers to add to his crews. The girl-employees were excellent home cooks; however, none knew about "mass" production of egg-rolls, especially in the quantities needed to meet the demand of the American market.

The Food and Drug Administration (FDA) closely inspected the quality of Can's products and scrutinized the labels on the boxes to make sure they were accurate and meeting the FDA requirements. Regularly, inspectors came from the County Health Department and the officials involved have never asked Can to do anything that was unreasonable. They always gave him enough time to take care of things.

Can made it a point to test and retest his products and follow up on the comments and criticisms offered candidly to him by his customers and friends. One of the most significant standards Can imposed was that each egg-roll made, had to have the exact same quality taste.

Can tried to market his products towards a number of Oriental food stores and American supermarkets. After special efforts, and in spite of some language difficulty, he succeeded in persuading some store-owners to sample his deep-fried egg-rolls. The tasty product sold itself instantly.

Currently some 15 percent of his business is done in sales from his modest retail outlet; 85 percent of the operations turn-over is wholesale. Can used relatively little advertising but worked hard by personally visiting customers and delivering the products to stores and restaurants, thus helping to consolidate his business contacts while at the same time he collected his bills and could improve his cash flow effectively. A friend of Can's recently developed two excellent routes for Can's business. The friend receive a 20 per cent discount and does his own routing. He now services about thirty stores and restaurants along with some colleges and high schools. Each delivery route is serviced once a week. The egg-rolls keep a minimum of fifteen days in a refrigerator or longer in a deep freezer.

Can likes to sell to the consumer in bulk since individual packaging is often as expensive as the ingredients. He is currently distributing the egg-rolls in cake boxes under his own label.

He took care of the bookkeeping, but used a Certified Public Accountant for the taxes and accounting. The CPA also gives advice on numerous financial matters, such as: loan applications, cost analysis, applying the proper mark up ratios, inventory maintenance and price adjustments.

Another necessary business need that had to be filled was insurance:  product liability, accident, workman's compensation, and fire and auto coverage.

In order to stay in business and to cope with other competitors' efforts, Can was fully aware of the fact that he must bring improvements to his overall outfit. As of the writing of this paper, the candidate just learned that Can had installed some modern food-manufacturing and packaging machinery at his new factory-site, and parallelly with this measure he had some sections of his operation computerized in order to update every stage of production and marketing.

The case of this young entrepreneur is one of success, typical among enterprising Vietnamese settlers in this country. Can's and other similar successes deserve close scrutiny and study by other newcomers, for this is an example of how a traditional native business can be developed and modernized thanks to new sophisticated equipment, efficient financing, updated business management and, above all, enthusiastic zeal of the entrepreneur himself and his willingness to improve and advance his business and business knowledge.

The writer strongly believes that if Can maintains his good business ethics and shows outstanding leadership with his collaborators, his business could expand and develop considerably in the months and years to come.

In addition to this line of business, that is, egg-roll manufacturing, we may add the production of meat pie (giò lụa), fish-ball and meat-ball (cá viên, bò viên), sour preserved pork (nem chua), shrimp-paste (mắm tôm) and anchovy sauce (mắm nêm)... Some of these food items are still being imported from Thailand, Taiwan, Hong Kong, and the Philippines. Eventually they could be produced in the States with modern procedures, qualified food engineers and shrewd business graduates from American colleges. When this happens, imagine what huge amounts of hard currency will be saved from the reduction of the importation of such food items, thus helping in cutting down the national budget deficit to some noticeable extent.

"New product development is an essential element in any corporation's growth and survival. It is essential because it is not uncommon for a major corporation to achieve more than 50 percent of its current sales in products which is less than five years old. And it is essential because ours is an economy in which competition, evolving technologies, and changing market needs make existing products obsolete more rapidly than ever before. Furthermore, it is clear that the nature of diversification of most United States industrial firms has changed dramatically over the past decade."[1]

"While there is no certainty in predicting new product failures, many could have been foretold. By and large, product development is marked by a low success ratio, a high mortality rate, tremendous costs, and low returns. Yet it is an indispensable arena, one in which most companies must not only compete, but must compete successfully in order to survive and grow."[2]

As time goes on, we see more and more oriental food-manufacturers being established in the major concentrated areas of Asian residents. For example, currently Can (the subject in the above case study) is not the only egg-roll manufacturer in Houston, there are at least three other outfits competing against one another all to the benefit of the consumers. Competition will bring about progress for all in this land of opportunity and free enterprise!

[1]*Carl E. Bochmann, "New Product Development," Handbook of Business Problem Solving," Kenneth J. Albert, Editor-in-Chief, MacGraw-Hill Book Co., New York, 1980, p.4-3.*
 [2]*Ibid. p.4-4. (See figure 1-1, p.127)*

# PROFIT GRAPH UTILIZATION

A profit graph or income realization chart—better known as a break-even chart—distinguishes and expresses cost-volume relationships, while distinguishing between fixed and variable costs. The profit graph attempts to explain how profits or revenues are affected by changes in sales volume. Although break-even analysis is a simple technique to use and understand. there are shortcomings to this method.

The break-even point (BEP) expressed in dollar sales can be estimated by using the following formula:

$$\text{BEP \$ (sales)} = \frac{\text{fixed costs (\$)}}{1 - \dfrac{\textit{variable costs} \text{ (unit sold)}}{\textit{selling price} \text{ (unit sold)}}}$$

$$\text{BEP \$} = \frac{F}{1 - \dfrac{v}{s}}$$

This can be shown geometrically as follows:

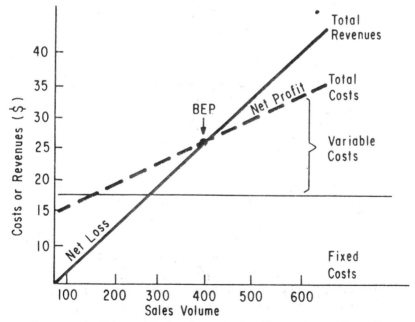

Source: A. Edward Spitz, "Marketing Resources: Allocation and Optimization", Petrocelli Books, New York, 1974, p. 90.

**New Products**

FIGURE 1-1
(a) Product Life-Cycle Curve (b) Life Cycle
for Faddish Product

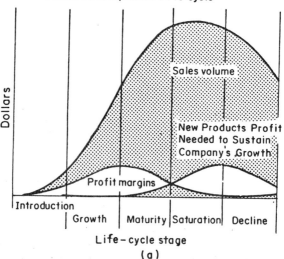

Sales volume curve and profit margin curve
in relation to a product's life cycle

(a)

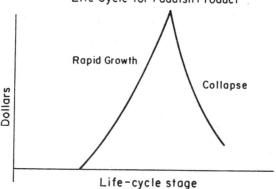

Life Cycle for Faddish Product

From HANDBOOK OF BUSINESS PROBLEM SOLVING,
McGraw-Hill Book Company, New York, 1970. Reproduced
by permission.

## 4. LAND DEVELOPMENT AND HOME BUILDING

Giang (the principal character in this case-study) is a well-known teacher and author of several series of textbooks which have educated and enlightened at least two generations of Vietnamese in North Vietnam (prior to the partition of the country in 1954) and in South Vietnam from 1956 to April 1975 when the communist onslaught spearheaded into Saigon. He was fortunate enough to be allowed to fly out of the devastated capital in a C-130 giant transport plane assigned by the U.S. Air Force to pick up families of the Vietnamese members of the International Control Commission (ICC) for fear of communists' astrocious reprisals against them.

He did not have any language barrier problem when he and his family settled down in this country after completing the required procedures in Fort Chaffee, Arkansas. He was exceptionally pragmatic and did not lose any time in educating himself in various new fields through the facilities offered by numerous educational institutions available in a cosmopolitan city like Houston, Texas. The Continuing Education Center of the University of Houston offers courses in business administration, insurance, real estate, investment, foreign languages, and so many other useful educational disciplines.

Giang spent three years acquiring as much knowledge as he could through eighteen different courses of study at the C.E.C. of the University of Houston, where he managed to get several diplomas with accreditation in subjects such as finance, economics, and management. This center also helped him with knowledge to pass the tough exam in obtaining his real estate broker's license which currently requires 900 class hours and a passing score of 80/100 for the difficult tests.

Knowing the essential fact that doing business, especially in an advanced capitalist country such as the U.S., a thorough understanding of financial management must have first priority, Giang never loses sight of the basic principle: "Financial management is not a totally independent area of business administration. Instead, it draws heavily on related disciplines and fields of study. The most important of these are accounting and economics; in the latter discipline, macroeconomics and microeconomics are of special significance. Marketing, production, and the study of quantitative methods also have an impact on the financial management field."[1]

Being armed with the necessary know-how in the various business activities in the new homeland in addition to his thirty-odd years of hard work and well-earned experience as an outstanding educator and businessman in his native country, Giang was ready to tackle a new stage in his life of ups and downs. His publishing operations and investment programs proved quite successful in all aspects. He even managed to make substantial gains in the unpredictable commodity futures exchange.

In his real estate investment, Giang succeeded in making a profit in the lower six figures in his first (1976) venture when he bought an apartment complex of 36 units in the Southeastern area of Houston. Later, in 1978, he was approached by two fellow Vietnamese, whom he did not know, but who were introduced to him by some priests and other elders.

In a way these individuals came to appeal for help in a new enterprise which concern the development of some real estate and construction of new homes on the site. Giang spent some time in going through the overall project and quickly came to

---

[1] *R. Charles Moyer, James R. McGuigan & William J. Kretlow, "Contemporary Financial Management," West Publishing Co., St. Paul, Mn., 1981, p. 4.*

the conclusion that he simply could not bail them out of the mess. He noticed that they were trying to set up a "Vietnamese Village" with the blessing of the priests. This was against Giang's concept as he had always advocated doing away with any sort of creation of a Vietnamese ghetto or Harlem in any part of this country. While all other ethnic groups are endeavoring to rid themselves of such racial conglomerations, in Giang's mind he saw no reason whatsoever for setting up a "Vietnamese Village" or "Vietnamese Parish," which is all nonsensical, entirely contradicting Giang's way of thinking.

On one occasion, in September, 1984, Giang had a chance to talk to a "Houston Post" newspaper reporter when asked of his opinion regarding the setting up of so-called "Vietnamese Villages," he had this to say: "The Vietnamese who segregate themselves in a village environment will surely miss getting into the mainstream of American society, which would help them in numerous ways in improving on their prospects. The concept of isolating oneself in a particular ethnic surrounding is absolutely obsolete."

The two individuals made complete concession and approached Giang once again by asking him to carry out what project he would like with the available tracts of land — almost 30 acres in total area. After two weeks of minutious negotiations, Giang accepted to be the chairman and chief executive officer of the new outfit for implementing the project of building 90 single home units on the first tract.

With Giang's relationship and reputation, he was able to strike a deal with a local savings and loan institution with which the new firm could transform the raw land into 90 home lots. The next step was to negotiate with his bank whose president and senior vice-president knew of Giang's credibility through previous financial transactions. There was not much difficulty in having the consent of the bank to approve of the interim loans for construction.

All went well to the amazement of Giang's American competitors in the neighborhood. In the first nine months, Giang's corporation managed to sell 51 homes making a profit of around $250,000 net... But greed blinded the conscience of the other shareholders who were holding 52 percent of the shares while Giang had only 48 percent and thus in the minority. Here came the turning point, one of the shareholders (call him Ly) — whose background Giang later found out was deplorable. Ly was an orphan that joined the Vietnamese army as a non-commissioned officer whose ethics was hopelessly worthy of condemnation. This individual, because of lack of morality, started dissension among the other associates in the real estate group. Ly constantly fomented trouble, started quarrels, screamed and shouted in meetings and showed all forms of rudeness and baseness to provoke Giang's anger in a way to get rid of him so as to have a greater share of the profit that was already foreseeable. Greed also influenced the other shareholders, who, to Giang's surprise, were ready to join Ly in overthrowing Giang.

It was obvious that a case of collusion to get Giang out of the picture was in the offing. Giang consulted his attorney and was advised to withdraw from the corporation. The remaining partners were more than glad to know of this ultimate decision because all they wanted was the ouster of Giang, since his role in arranging the loans was over. All legal documents were prepared by attorneys of both parties and Giang got back his capital as well as the prorated profits at that stage of the operations.

"Man proposes, God disposes" so runs the proverb. Things did not turn out so nicely and smoothly as expected by the all remaining shareholders. Only one month after Giang left the entity, the bank rate began to skyrocket until it reached 21.5 percent. No new homes could be sold. Meanwhile, instead of trimming expenses, and when most other colleagues had to suspend work or declare bankruptcy, the remaining partners each bought a Mercedes-Benz car and hired an additional secretary just to "save face."

In only 14 months after Giang's withdrawal from the corporation the company closed down with the result that they lost their entire capitals and profits to the extent of nearly half a million dollars.

The moral of this particular case is: as far as technology and modern business practices were concerned, everything went on all right. The great mistake made by Giang was that he just took the friends' referrals for granted without making detailed investigations of his prospective business partners. It served Giang a good lesson of cautiousness and prudence: "Never to associate in business dealings with anyone whose complete background is unknown or only vaguely known."

Was this a typical example of failure? Yes, a failure in morality and trust. A failure to realize that among the Vietnamese refugee-immigrants there are also crooks. So, investors beware!

But in terms of financial profit, Giang gained a rather good sum from this "unfortunate" venture. He only felt saddened at the wickedness, meanness, and indignity of his former partners. One undeniable fact is that all the Vietnamese in not only the local community but elsewhere have looked down upon and shunned away from those criminal-conscious "sharks and piranhas."

The concept of setting up "Vietnamese Villages" has proven itself to be absolutely sectarian and outdated, as similar projects were tried and failed in Houston, New Orleans, Orange County, San Jose, and a number of other areas. One of the main causes of this heart-breaking failure (with some honest advocators losing their fortunes) is that none of the developers had any thorough knowledge of modern business administration nor of the recent racial trend in this country, also not understanding the several social problems involved in such projects. The U.S. is today an open society advocating interracial harmony in its progress and development, while sporadic cases of discrimination may occur, as these progressive laws are being popularized and enforced.

Quite a few newcomers have tried their hands in land development and home construction, for there is ready demand in the various communities. Those who are reckless and poorly equipped with the required knowledge fail utterly while those who are well armed with sophisticated know-how in the various business phases and trends, and those who are respected and trusted by their fellowmen succeed. Again, entrepreneurs beware!

## 5. THE MEDICAL PROFESSIONS

Among the Vietnamese expatriates who had chosen the United States as their second homeland as a consequence of the downfall of Saigon, capital of the defunct Republic of Vietnam, in Spring 1975, it is commonly acknowledged that physicians, dentists and pharmacists were the most fortunate and priveleged group because they were among the few professionals who could carry on their former trades in this new land, though their academic background is not extraordinarily far above people of other walks of life.

Under the French colonialization era (1865-1945) little was done in the medical field for the benefit of the Indochinese. During World War I, when the French metropolitan government could not send over physicians and paramedics to its overseas possessions, it started the medical faculty in Hanoi, North Vietnam, with the objective of turning out a very restricted number of Indochinese "medecin" (medical assistants) whose medical knowledge and training were quite below international standards. Only until the outbreak of World War II (1939) did the French raise the academic criteria of the faculties of medicine and pharmacy to the metropolitan (meaning French) status.

The Indochinese physicians, dentists and pharmacists who graduated in 1945 and later years had the required international standards, but those who graduated as of 1958 and the subsequent years were mostly trained and taught in the Armed Forces Medical School to funnel into the military medical corps for emergency field services which reached its climax in the second phase of the Vietnam War (1964-1975). Training courses were often through "crash" programs, but the newly graduated medical officers had immediate field services and on-the-job training and experiences.

When those ex-medical officers arrived in the U.S. in 1975, they were offered special considerations to help them get back to their former professions and partly, too, to provide medical care for the hundreds of thousands of Indochinese refugees who could communicate more easily with their "national" medical cadres.

After the English language test, that is English as a second language, the criterion of which is equivalent to the TOEFL test* required for freshmen's admission to most colleges such as Houston, Rice, Stanford, Cornell, Duke... They would have to pass a basic test on medical background and terminology. An average Vietnamese general-practice physician (such as Drs. CBH, LQH, HVM...) took only less than a year of preparation to pass all the academic requirements and was licensed by the State Board of Medical Examiners to practice their profession officially like any American-trained physician.

Indochinese-trained physicians, once admitted as refugees into the U.S., are categorized as parolees under a special ordinance, and in this capacity they have, in some respect, privileges over other foreign physicians, also called FMGs (Foreign Medical Graduates). In addtition to the English language test, they have to pass the FLEX[1] and ECFMG[2] tests. But in the aftermath of the phony MD diplomas scandal that exploded in 1983 when the FBI booked Pedro de Mesones, a naturalized American of Peruvian origin, for selling bogus medical diplomas and receiving over $1.5 million, and the Medi-Cal Scam in California by mid-February 1984, the AMA began to have a rigid and severe attitude towards the FMGs, especially the non-white FMGs, including those from

*TOEFL: Test of English as a Foreign Language
[1]Federal Licensing Examination
[2]Educational Council for Foreign Medical Graduates

Indochina. The most recent medical arrivals have to bear the unfortunate consequences caused by their forerunners.

In a way, it is an accepted fact that while the American medical student had to toil and moil for several years in pre-med and medical schools in addition to tough and severe internship, the newly-arrived physicians had the chance to practice the profession in this country through a "circumstantial piece of good luck." So much the better for the Indochinese physician as well as for the Indochinese refugees, because the latter, due to language barrier, needed their native physicians, dentists and even pharmacists. The refugees are appreciative that the U.S. Government reserved such facilities and privileges to the newly-arrived medical practitioners, for those lenient measures were also directly contributing helpful services to the Indochinese settlers all over the country.

Averagedly speaking, most of the medical practitioners could pass the board exams in a period of two years at most. Consequently by 1977-1978, the number of licensed physicians and dentists of Vietnamese origin in this country practicing their former professions was considerable and conspicuous in most Vietnamese communities, and 60 percent of the ads on Vietnamese-language papers and magazines were relevant to those new medical and dental outfits. (It is wondered whether this excessive ads practice is in conformity with good ethics.)

Normally, most of them were making good incomes much higher than all other newcomers, while the intellectuals of other professions such as lawyers, engineers, architects, journalists, teachers, artists, bankers, and in particular the ex-servicemen had to learn new trades[3]. Quite a few of the latter had to accept menial jobs to make both ends meet due to poor knowledge of English that is essentially required in the new

---

[3]*Ref. to "New Life of Overseas Vietnamese," p. 74.*

land.   In addition to the lucrativeness of the medical professions, the U.S. Government brought a financial windfall to this already existing jackpot: social welfare, Medicare, and Medicaid programs.   The Indochinese pharmacists were also reaping their "greenback crops" thanks to sales of tons of medical drugs that found their way from various Vietnamese communities in the U.S. to Communist-ruled Vietnam, shipped to a thriving black market as well as to the relatives and friends of expatriates living in the various communities in the United States. "The drugs can be life-saving humanitarian gifts, but for black market operations - they mean inflated profits.  Even non-prescription American-made drugs such as aspirin and decongestants, are hot sellers on the Vietnamese black market".[4]

There are, of course, **a great number of ethical, honest, and conscientious Vietnamese medical practitioners who respect the laws and regulations**, and above all, **who are imbued with humanitarian consideration for their compatriots. For these respectable professionals the author shares the admiration and homage of his fellow-countryfolks.**   Some Vietnamese physicians would brave the rigid weather, through blizzards and storms, to care for needy patients, not minding whether the latter could afford to pay them or not; they are true models of the humanitarian life-savers.

But unfortunately in Spring 1984, a huge scandalous bombshell exploded in broad daylight in the state of California.   In later years, if we were asked which was the most detrimental and disgraceful happening among the Vietnamese newcomers during their first decade in the U.S., the immediate answer would be the Medi-Cal Scams.   And because of its significance, the author feels that some account should be included in this study to mark a sad and shameful episode of

---

[4]*Cook, Chuck, staff writer of "The Register," Orange County, Ca., Feb. 1984.*

the Vietnamese pioneering efforts in the Land of Justice and Freedom. Furthermore, it is hoped that this embittered incident also serves as a moral lesson to our children and their children that "greed is abominable" and "honesty is always the best policy."

In writing the account herebelow, the candidate wishes to acknowledge with thanks the journalists who reported detailed narrations on the "Medi-Cal Scams" during the critical moments of the occurrence.

Sweeping through some minority communities from San Jose to San Diego, a special task force arrested 45 people on February 15, 1984, including doctors, dentists, and pharmacists, who allegedly bilked the Medi-Cal programs of at least 27.5 million dollars. Carrying search warrants, dozens of investigators from local Orange County and state agencies went rounding up suspects, documents and goods allegedly purchased illegally with Medi-Cal stickers.

Arrests were made in Orange County, San Diego, Los Angeles and Santa Clara counties. Charges included falsifying Medi-Cal claims, grand theft, conspiracy and paying kickbakcs. Conviction would carry a maximum three-year jail sentence and $5,000 fine. Bail ranged from $11,000 for so-called "drivers" who ran errands for doctors - such as delivering Medi-Cal stickers and payments - to $250,000 for the suspects who were most heavily involved.

"The reactions to the arrests displayed splits within the Vietnamese community. Some lauded the arrests, thinking it was time to put an end to abuses of public funds; others expressed fear that the arrests would prompt anti-Vietnamese feelings among the public."[5]

---

[5]Cook, Chuck and Steven R. Churm, "The Register," Orange County, Cal., February 16, 1984.

Most Vietnamese residents in the Orange County, when interviewed, made known that those malicious elements, especially those who considered themselves intellectuals belonging to the "top wealthy new class in their adopted homeland" got snatched red-handed should examine their conscience in closer scrutiny for having brought shame upon their fellow countryman.

It was recently learned that Medicare spending restrictions advocated by the Administration were beginning to hurt quite a few needy and elderly patients and were undoubtedly the consequence of the high incidence of Medi-Cal fraud uncovered during the California Medi-Cal Scams. The federal government would certainly impose drastic changes in the refugee-assistance program that has helped 650,000 Southeast Asians settle in the United States since 1975. Bob Evans, inspector general of the U.S. Department of Health and Human Services' regional office in San Francisco, said that the overall operation of the program would be reviewed.[6]

Carla Singer, attorney general of Orange County made known that 34 fraudulent providers were paid more than $7.2 million in Medi-Cal funds in 1983, adding that investigators hoped materials seized in the searches would tell what percentage, if any, of each provider's billings were fraudulent. Arrests had to be made simultaneously so that words of the investigations would not leak out.[7]

The majority of the Vietnamese residents in Orange County and Los Angeles County felt indignant and frustrated on knowing of the wrongdoings committed by such a number of "intellectuals" who were blinded by greed and temptations of materialistic luxuries. They believed that the local people would distinguish the good and honest elements from the

---

[6]*Ibid.*
[7]*Tripoli, staff writer of the "Los Angeles Times," Feb. 1984.*

unethical few. As the months passed by (already a full year), what they had hoped for became a reality: the people (non-Vietnamese) still maintain friendly relationship with all the law-abiding newcomers and no incident of grudge, provocation or enmity has occurred. The racial harmony among the citizens in those two counties was perfectly maintained.

In fact, the Medi-Cal Scams started with complaints from the Vietnamese themselves. Investigations were carried out in Santa Ana, Garden Grove, San Jose, Los Angeles and San Diego. Police said they could not have made the first step without support from the Vietnamese people themselves. This proved that the Vietnamese in general are law-abiding and respect justice in all circumstances. Only a very small minority would go astray and infringe upon the laws.

State officials became aware of the Medi-Cal Scams in late 1981 after members of the Vietnamese community complained that some doctors, dentists and pharmacists were bilking the health care program. In 1982, other police agencies also began receiving reports alleging widespread abuses. The formal investigation began after state Medi-Cal fraud investigators met with Washington Police Chief Jack Shuckley in April 1983.

It is unnecessary to go into further details concerning this case which leaves a long-lasting scar on the Vietnamese communities. The medical professionals, like any other Vietnamese people, are running their businesses for a living, but let them carry on their trades according to good ethics and the code of the medical profession, and they can win the respect of their fellow-countryfolks.

This scandàl will have its place in the history of the Vietnamese pioneers in the United States. Like all other ethnic groups that have settled in this country, there are a few despicable elements while the majority are dignified honest people who work hard for their decent livelihood.

In this professional category associated with the Vietnamese settlers we could include acupuncturists, chiropractors, Oriental medicinal herbalists... who *normally are highly respected by their fellow-countrymen*. This is partly due to Confucian teaching that reserves special regards for the healing professionals, as it has been believed that they are the ones that could restore life to afflicted individuals. The Vietnamese term "bác sĩ" literally means *"an intellectual of erudite learning"*, which is usually preferred to "y-sĩ" (the intellectual who cures), "nha-sĩ" (the intellectual who heals decayed teeth), "dược-sĩ" (the intellectual who deals in medications), "đông-y-sĩ" (the Oriental medicinal herbalist), and so forth. But if some of these intellectuals bring disgrace on the Vietnamese community as in the case discussed above they (that shameful minority) will be scorned at. The reward is great; however, the damnation is also severe.

# VIETNAMESE REFUGEE-PAROLEES
## ADMITTED TO THE U.S.A. (1975-80)

| 1975-1980 | 1980 | 1979 | 1978 | TQ1976 | 1976 | 1975 |
|---|---|---|---|---|---|---|
| 244,414 | 53,392 | 53,121 | 14,358 | 1854 | 85,396 | 34,946 |

## INITIAL ADMISSIONS OF VIETNAMESE REFUGEES
### Immigration and Naturalization Sce

| | Current Month Total | Cumula. Fisc. Yr. Total | Current Month Prin.Ref. | Cumula. Fisc.Yr. Prin.Ref. | Current Month Spouse of Ref. | Cumula. Cum. Spouse of Ref. | Current Month Child. of Ref. | Cum. FY Child. of Ref. |
|---|---|---|---|---|---|---|---|---|
| Sept. 1982 | 3698 | 40,604 | 2054 | 22,553 | 340 | 4725 | 1304 | 13,346 |
| Sept. 1983 | 2695 | 21,463 | 1463 | 11,584 | 268 | 2101 | 964 | 7,778 |
| Mar. 1984 | 2793 | 12,090 | 1436 | 6,207 | 309 | 1238 | 1048 | 4,545 |

146

TABLE

Refugee Cash Assistance Utilization Rates (Calculated with Different
Methodologies) for the Ten States with the Largest Refugee
Populations in 1980 and 1983

| STATE | TOTAL REFUGEE POPULATION JANUARY, 1980 (1) | 1980 DATA TOTAL REFUGEE RECIPIENT POPULATION AUG 1, 1980 (2) | COLUMN 1 ÷ COLUMN 2 (3) | 1983 DATA PERCENTAGE OF TIME-ELIGIBLE POPULATION RECEIVING ASSISTANCE (4) |
|---|---|---|---|---|
| California | 85,938 | 73,800 | 86.9% | 91% |
| Texas | 23,692 | 7,803 | 33.0 | 15 |
| Washington | 10,773 | 12,394 | 115.0 | 45 |
| Pennsylvania | 10,504 | 5,195 | 49.0 | 57 |
| Illinois | 8,899 | 7,258 | 82.0 | 40 |
| Virginia | 8,092 | 3,870 | 48.0 | 30 |
| Louisiana | 7,592 | 2,893 | 38.0 | 29 |
| Minnesota | 7,225 | 9,852 | 136.0 | 64 |
| New York | 6,670 | 2,649 | 40.0 | 42 |
| Oregon | 6,462 | 7,058 | 109.0 | 53 |

Sources: Columns 1 and 2, Office of Refugee Resettlement; Report to Congress, January 31, 1981, Tables 10 and 14; Column 4, preliminary ORR data for September 30, 1983.

Note: Since the 1980 Amendments had not come into effect on either of the dates in 1980, data are for what now would be called time-eligible Indochinese refugees. The 1983 data cover both Indochinese and non-Indochinese refugees. Data for both years cover ORR-funded assistance programs only (which excludes, for example, Food Stamps).

## 6. THE RICE NOODLE SOUP SHOP

Description of the Business

If hot dogs and hamburgers are the Americans' most popular fast-food items, the rice noodle soup (phở) definitely deserves to be their counterpart among the Vietnamese.[1] This food item originated from the Chinese rice noodle soup which is very simple in term of ingredients and preparation, but the Vietnamese "phở" is recognized by all to be much more sophisticated and consequently more delicious than the original Chinese soup.

Prior to the partition of Vietnam along the 17th parallel in July, 1954, the rice noodle soup (phở) was only popular in North Vietnam, and that is why it is also called "phở Bắc" meaning the "Northern noodle soup". But when nearly two million refugees moved from North Vietnam to South Vietnam in the aftermath of the Geneva Agreement, this food item was immediately welcomed by the Southern Vietnamese.

The Know-how

Sinh, a Northern Vietnamese, happened to come from a family that had, for at least two generations, run a "phở" shop in Hanoi, North Vietnam, prior to 1954 and eventually a new shop in Saigon, when they migrated and resettled in their new home, in South Vietnam. The rice noodle soup shop provided his parents with sufficient income to raise seven children (three boys and four girls), now all grown ups. Sinh's sisters were all married, while two of his brothers were University of Saigon graduates, but he himself lagged behind with only a high school diploma.

---

[1]Please read *"New Life of Overseas Vietnamese,"* p. 74.

Sinh was wise enough to have learned the trade from his parents, that is, the "secret" formulas and recipes for preparing superb rice noodle soups. Once settled in Garden Grove, California, he was immediately in search of a suitable but inexpensive location to set up a noodle shop that would let him be his own boss. He was convinced that with a very modest capital - just $2,000 - he could set up his new shop and make enough money to support himself and his family of four. He would also have the additional satisfaction of providing useful service to his fellow-countryfolks as his noodle shop would serve as a sort of meeting place for quite a few Vietnamese in the neighborhood.

The Decision

So he was well on his way...

Sinh was a gregarious type of person and was truly fond of people - especially his customers. He always made them feel they were welcome, and in this manner he indeed fulfilled the first rule for the successful business operation. Fortunately, his efficient wife was as businesslike as he was, and she never felt demeaned by working behind the counter and would gladly take orders from customers.

The Location

A suitable location for his business was the most important decision he had to make. His shop must be in a densely populated part of the city where the Vietnamese residents would come regularly, as he was aware that his regular customers would be walk-ins. So he had to select his neighborhood carefully.

## Rules and Regulations

Sinh was smart enough to build up good relations with the Health Department and the police, and both could tip him off to possible problems in advance, when asked.

## The Installation

When the couple started business in Garden Grove, California, they leased a modest store only about 1000 square feet with sufficient space for kitchen layout and room for twenty-odd seats. The decor was simple with a rustic North Vietnamese theme that is liked by all his patrons.

## Decors

The next major step now was to turn the bare interior into the warm, inviting spot he saw in his mind's eye.

The kitchen was the heart of his efficient operation. It should be well equipped for his business, but at the same time Sinh had a tight budget outlay so he would buy only the essentials, then accumulate the supply gradually.

## The Capital

The capital required for opening a rice noodle soup shop is not large. It all depends on how the owner wanted his store to be: large or small, fancy or simple... It could be a modest capital of a few hundred dollars to thousands of dollars. An ad asking for free chairs and a swing through the area's garage sales should solve the "seating" problem for one owner while another shop-owner would prefer all brand new furniture! The most essential requirements for a successful noodle store are: friendly attitude of the owner and the superb quality of his soups and ingredients!

Cleanliness

Our friend Sinh always sees to it that the toilets are light and clean - the restrooms are always spotless. Nothing turns people off faster than dirty johns.

Characteristics

Another characteristic worthy of notice and praise at Sinh's shop is that it had a medium-sized bulletin board on which were notices, bulletins, announcements, short ads... concerning the local Vietnamese community. He also had a newsstand for sale of Vietnamese-language papers and magazines. In this way, his customers had a feeling that they were coming to a club house to enjoy delicious noodle soup, gather information, and exchange some gossips with friends all at once.

Personnel and Management.

As for the personnel problems, Sinh would not be able to afford many employees at the starting stage, but at least two were a definite necessity. The first - a bookkeeper - was a must so that he might know where he stood, and he would not have trouble later with the IRS and local tax agencies. The second employee should be a cleanup person who would scrub the place down every morning. Once his business picked up, he could hire waiters or waitresses, but he always remembered that to run his store efficiently he and his wife must be able to do all of his employees' jobs well. Sinh also knew that one of the best ways to form a loyal, efficient staff was to pay the going rates and to let his employees know what he was making and give them a share of the rewards of good business.

## The Food and Drink

So far, nothing had been said about the food and drink Sinh offered to his customers. Like the menu in a hamburger shop, that in a rice noodle soup shop contains only a few items, ordinarily not more than ten items including the beverages. So, this limited menu is often painted conspicuously on a board or printed on a menu.

He also invited his patrons to try some specialties of his shop, such as: flan (custard) with rum, French pastries, various traditional coffees and dishes... some of which were being supplied by outside caterers. The specialties he served should be a sort of feature of his shop as distinctive from other shops. Furthermore, pastries and cakes - if good ones were available - were also profitable items to handle.

## Marketing

Sinh would regularly check what his competition was charging so as to be certain that he was not overpricing or underpricing. All his costs must be covered or he would soon be out of business. He also spent a reasonable amount of money to start his publicity campaign with a good location and a big sign. He would move along his guests and ask them what they liked and disliked about the new establishment. In this way, he could get lots of free advice, some of it quite useful, as he strongly believed in the old saying: "Your best advertisement is a satisfied customer."

*Remarks*

Although Sinh has never been to a business school, yet the various steps he has taken in setting up and running his rice noodle soup shop are close to the criteria required for managing a small business destined for success. Again, if Sinh feels complacent with his current income and business operations, he could be assured to stay in business for some time to come. However, if he wants to expand his operations with some additional shops as a way to start a small-scale chain of stores, he would have to acquire more knowledge in modern business administration.

This category of business also comprises the following: small restaurants, Oriental eateries, ice cream parlors, soda fountains, luncheon shops... which are mostly family-run outfits basing on traditional know-how and experience handed down from parents to children. The very moment some key persons in the family feel bored with the business, they would give it up by selling it out to another party. Very often we find that children of such store-owners - when they attain higher academic levels, such as: law, engineering, architecture, sciences... would like to quit the family-run eating-house. Quite a few stores, used to be owned by American Born Chinese (ABC) in California, for instance, were sold to newly-arrived Vietnamese and Chinese Vietnamese in the years 1975 to 1982, for the very reasons elaborated above. Then in turn, the first refugees who came in 1975 would be selling their outfits to recently arrived refugees, as the former's children acquire higher academic diplomas. This proves a point that most of the so-called "pop and mom" businesses are time-consuming and boring. Since the owners must use their own time and labor to earn their living.

From the classified ads section on the Vietnamese-language "Thuong Mai" (Commerce) weekly magazine, published in Houston, Texas, March 7, 1985 issue, the candidate counted 88 ads for sales of small businesses among the Vietnamese in Houston alone. This illustrates that a great number of stores have changed hands rather frequently, which is not a good omen for prosperity and development. It has also been commented that the higher the unemployment rate rises the more small businesses open, because the Vietnamese "laid-offs" were anxious to use their hard-earned savings to "go into business" without possessing any business background or proper investigations. The regrettable result was that over 85% of them failed miserably; some solutions, practical and efficient, must be brought about to remedy this tragic situation.

As competition becomes keener, business failures will also increase accordingly, if the small businesspeople stick to their traditional trades and professions. For example, in the case of the noodle shop just described above, if only one shop opens, it can gain financial rewards so easily. But then, other people will follow suit, and several additional noodle shops would also want to share the "lucrative" market... until the situation reached the point of saturation in a short period of time. Then there would be severe competition such as price cutting, unfair promotional gimmicks, and other underhand tricks that could be harmful to one another. Needless to say, someone would get hurt if the vicious circle was allowed to go on unchecked and unsolved.

This is truly a "boom and gloom" situation. The free-for-all competition will eventually lead to self-destruction.

"Two closely related functions of managing are *planning* and *controlling*. Planning looks to the future; controlling checks the past. The two, thus, serve as perspectives for the manager who makes decisions in the present."[1].

---

[1]*Joseph L. Massie, "Essentials of Management," 2nd ed., Prentice-Hall, Englewood Cliffs, N.J., 1971, p. 82*

## 7. THE CONVENIENCE STORE BUSINESS

Anyone from a developed or undeveloped country is familiar with the "mom and pop" grocery store, which in Vietnamese is called "tiệm tạp hóa" meaning "miscellaneous store" or "sundry foodstore." The overseas Chinese in South-East Asian countries (Vietnam, Cambodia, Laos, Thailand, Malaysia, Indonesia, the Philippines) are well-known for running such stores, because the essential requirements to maintain such an outfit is hard work, hard work, hard work! The capital outlay is minimal while the language barrier problem could be overcome after a short period of time because of the limited vocabulary demanded.

When the Vietnamese refugees first arrived in the United States, most of them were handicapped with lack of capital and especially because of the language barrier. However, the phenomenon of the convenience store presented to them was a God-sent boon to help them (under such pressing circumstances) to get started in earning their living in the new land.

In some states, the parent companies such as Southland Corporation (Seven-Eleven Stores), National Convenience Stores (Stop and Go), Circle K Corporation (Circle K stores)... required deposits amounting to somewhere around $10,000 or more per store, but in Texas, no deposit was required. So, thanks to this favorable condition, a great number of Indochinese families felt they had the ideal manpower and capability of handling the overall management and operation of the convenience store. They usually had the husband and wife team plus help from teenage children, no capital outlay required, modest fluency in English, some notion of written English for filling out requisition slips and record-keeping, and above all, the store-manager feels a sort of "independence" with no one continually looking over his shoulder as long as the family members work hard and render a good job to the corporation. In winter, they work in a well heated store and in summer, they work in cool air-conditioned atmosphere. The average income for the team (usually two persons on the payroll) working in an 18-hour store (6 a.m. to midnight) was about $1,800 per month (in 1976-79) with some fringe benefits, and undoubtedly the income could be more in 1985 dollars ($2,400 to $3,200 per month).

This modest income was relatively comfortable for a medium Vietnamese refugee family, and since most Vietnamese people advocate the "extended family" tradition, that is, children (even married ones) would live with their parents under the same roof, their savings have been substantial compared to American families with equal but individual earnings. Living this way, the majority of Vietnamese families could afford to send their children to colleges by defraying all expenses from the family common coffer. According to the most recent statistics published by the Department of Human Resources in its 1983 and 1984 reports, we know of some interesting figures.[1]

Some families are still working for the giant chains while others, after learning the ins and outs of the trade, are running stores of their own. In the latter case, we again witness some individuals crowned with success while others struck with heart-breaking failures.

"Most decisions in business involve a certain amount of risk. The ablest businessman, like the ablest poker players, know how to take risks in the game spirit. Having determined on a course, they stop weighing pros and cons, and concentrate

---

[1]*See Tables on pp. 160 & 161, 180-186.*

on strategy and action. Firmness of decision, by clearing the mind and strengthening the morale, is an important factor in a job switch. With good timing, strong preparation, and initial secrecy, firmness can go far to assure a successful outcome."[2]

Those Vietnamese who follow closely modern business management criteria as already mentioned in previous circumstances (pp. 113-128) naturally fare better, especially those who took the trouble to learn from their former American "bosses" are now familiar with the methods of financing, the sources of supplies, the overall management, as well as the marketing techniques. They could succeed fairly well. On the other hand, those who were still being handicapped by insufficient knowledge of updated business procedures, lack of necessary capital, absence of experience, frail health and age problems... would fail disastrously. Furthermore, there are constantly business "sharks and piranhas" preying on these pitiful naive people who would wish to try their hands in business with the hard-earned savings accumulated during the recent years.[3]

Those merciless "sharks" would pick up run-down or obsolete stores liquidated at dirt-cheap prices by the major chains. The sharks in turn repainted the old equipment and appliances as well as refurbish the entire store with a fresh coat of paint and put in some fixtures so as to give the run-down stores a "new look". They then advertise in Vietnamese-language newspapers and magazines for sale of "the once-in-a-lifetime bargain" with yearly return on investment (ROI) of 40% to 50% (!). The poor pitiful and naive prospective investors got hooked and would lose their shirts! Too often the victims did not make sufficient investigation before they invested their entire savings in such ventures. The "bargain" convenience stores are typical example of the ruses which the

[2]Albert Z. Carr, "Business as a Game," New American Library, New York, 1968, p. 60.
[3]Please read "New Life of Overseas Vietnamese," on pp. 74-82.

"sharks and piranhas" use to lure their preys.

The victims did not possess even the very basic notion of cost reckoning, the various permits required by law, installation expenditures, maintenance of expensive items such as walk-in coolers, refrigerators, freezers, the clauses in the lease, state and federal taxes, deposits for phone and utilities... All of these demand a lot of cash, and if they did not have a "cushion" while building up their clientele, how long could they last before going bankrupt?

Nguyen, a typical successful man in the C-store (convenience store) business, was a former lieutenant in the Vietnamese Air Force ten years ago. He came to this country penniless and had to work as a manager at a Seven-Eleven store for four long years. After building up his nest-egg (1980), he took over an existing store in a "black" area, paying less than $5,000 cash for "everything." Through his store renovations and with exceptionally hard work, he turned the once not-so-profitable business around in less than a year. He made it his policy to treat every chance drop-in as a guest and wanted to please the customer as long as his store was open. He wanted to be sure that every customer could say of his C-store: "I go there" instead of "I've been there."

Another of Nguyen's smart tactics is that he keeps close observations on the progress and development advocated by the giant chains so as to learn from them. He keeps track of the updated window displays, the changing decors, the arrangement of the breakfast counter... and imitates the improvements while correcting the shortcomings. He has devoted all his energies and thoughts in the development of his life-time business, because that is the road he has chosen to build up his fortune in this land of opportunities.

At the time of the author's interview with Nguyen, he announced that he and a couple of associates had set up a small chain of four stores and hopefully by the end of this decade (the 80's), the business could extend to ten additional locations *if* nothing destructive and disharmonious would come in the way of progress.

While there are rewards in the C-store business, there are also numerous dangers, risks and hazards. It is said the a C-store manager or employee runs even greater perils than a police officer on active duty. Some are fortunate enough to have been spared any form of assaults and barbarous actions by felonious drug-addicts or criminals. However, the number of victims has been on the increase these recent years. Certainly this type of job is routine, perilous, low-paying and definitely not exciting in any manner. But in spite of its misgivings, some people took tremendous courage to accept the job and did some soul searching before coming to the final decision of running a C-store.

The author believes that up to a certain stage a person is so used to the routine work that he or she does not really care much about those aspects any more. However, it would not be long before he (the employee) would be listless and callous, wondering if he should have accepted the job in the first place. But as long as he has to keep the wolf from the door, he will have to get used to circumstances like the stuntmen who are confronting death practically every day of their lives and yet sometimes they even "enjoy" their jobs.[4]

In the category of the C-stores, we may include the following businesses: grocery stores, Oriental food stores, liquor stores, jewelry shops, gift shops, mini-supermarkets, sandwich stands, po-boy stores, tea-rooms, game-rooms, hot-

---

[4]*Appendix B, "Angel of Death Ends Dream," Houston Post, March 1985,* Houston, Texas, p. 8B.

dog booths, and pawn-shops... They are small businesses popularly known in Asian countries, but they have so many new additional and different characteristics when being operated in the U.S. and Canada. The utmost unique characteristic is that employees of those businesses are the most vulnerably victimized and brutalized by ruthless robbers, which brings us to the conclusion that earning a decent living in the new homeland is indeed tough and intricate.

"The man who gets ahead in business is the man who knows what he wants - and what he is willing to give up in order to get it," remarked the late Lord Beaverbrook in a speech. Inside this pithy utterance is a more complex truth. The man who has a clear vision of his goals is in a superior position to judge whether a given chance that comes his way is an opportunity that might carry toward those goals, or a temptation that would lead him astray.[5]

Almost every businessman has four major goals that he would like to reach - goals which add up to "success" in his mind - wealth, power, prestige, and security.[6]

---

[5]*"Business as a Game," p. 168.*
[6]*Ibid.*

Table    Characteristics of Grocery Stores, 1983

|  | Food Cooperatives | Profit-Oriented Stores |
|---|---|---|
| Number | 16 | 12 |
| Average Initial Investment | $20,000 | $32,000 |
| Average Monthly Sales | $ 5,400 | $19,400 |
| Paid Employees [1] | 9 | 12 |
| Clientele - Hmong | 74% | 56% |
|       - Other | 26% | 55% |
| Financial Status - Loss | 21% | — |
|       - Break Even | 43% | 40% |
|       - Profit | 26% | 60% |

[1] Includes full-time and part-time employees.

Table    Characteristics of Other Small Businesses, 1982-83

| Type of Enterprise | Investors | Initial Investment ($) | Monthly Sales ($) | Paid Employees[9] | Clientele (%) Hmong | Clientele (%) Other | Financial Status Loss | Even | Profit |
|---|---|---|---|---|---|---|---|---|---|
| Bakery[1] | 1 | 15,000 | — | 1 | 0 | 100 | | | x |
| Credit Union[1] | — | — | — | 0 | 100 | — | | x | |
| Supermarket/Wholesale Disc.[2] | 11 | 200,000 | 130,000 | 13 | 25 | 75 | | | x |
| Security Guard Service[3] | 3 | 350,000 | 60,000 | 50 | 0 | 100 | | | x |
| Restaurant[4] | | 80,000 | 20,000 | 7 | 0 | 100 | | | x |
| Restaurant[4] | 6 | 60,000 | 22,000 | 11 | 0 | 100 | | | x |
| Community Theatre | 2 | 10,000 | 1,500 | 0 | 100 | 0 | | x | |
| Jeweler[5] | 21 | 10,000 | 399 | 1 | 50 | 50 | | x | |
| Wood Crafts[6] | — | 3,000 | — | 2 | 0 | 100 | x | | |
| Toy Assembly[7] | 1 | 5,000 | 40,000 | 60 | 0 | 100 | | x | |
| Cleaning Service[8] | — | 2,000 | — | 2 | 0 | 100 | x | | |
| TOTAL (average) | 45 | 736,000 | 274,000 | 147 | (23) | (77) | 2 | 4 | 5 |

Notes:
1. Credit Union has 200 Hmong depositors and functions as non-profit service.
2. Eleven major investors provided initial $140,000. The balance came from 200 small contributors.
3. Two of the investors, providing almost all of the initial capital, were American.
4. The two restaurants belong to the same group of six investors.
5. Operates out of a grocery store.
6. Three hundred members of two Rotary Clubs provided initial support.
7. Operated as sub-contractor in toy factory for six months of 1982.
8. Funded by State as training grant. Venture dormant in mid-1983.
9. Includes full-time and part-time employees.

## 8. THE PUBLISHING BUSINESS

This particular case-study comprises the three following sections because they are interrelated:

A. Publishing (in its strict sense)
B. The Mail Order
C. The Cultural Store

## A. The Publishing Business

The publishing business pertains to the world of books. This line of business for Tam was started in Hanoi, North Vietnam, when he completed the compilation of the first English-Vietnamese Dictionary of Vietnam in 1949. The English language was adopted by a very small number of Vietnamese people as French was then the official medium in his country.

No one would care to publish such a book whose market was indeed thought to be quite limited. Tam carried his manuscript from one publisher to another, but everywhere he was shown a cold shoulder until he finally had to borrow a modest amount of 5,000 piasters (equivalent to U.S. $120 in 1949) from a "friend" who charged him 4% monthly or 48% per annum. With that initial fund, he launched himself into the publishing business by turning out 1,200 copies for distribution in North Vietnam as well as in South Vietnam under French control.

To his amazement, the first printing was so warmly welcomed by the Vietnamese public that in only four months, he had to produce a second printing of an additional run of 2,000 copies. This demand manifested the thirst of the

Vietnamese people, although living under the French expeditionary forces' strict rules, to be in search of other cultural horizons, especially Anglo-Saxon thoughts. With patience, Tam knew that paper and words could be built into a lucrative business along with his newly established language school.

The first publication (English-Vietnamese Dictionary) was soon followed by its complementary section: the "Vietnamese-English Dictionary" co-authored by Tam and his brother Phan. The two titles were instant best-sellers while Tam was bold enough to negotiate with Hachette, one of the largest French publishing firms to turn out a series of guides for their English-language textbooks aiming specially at helping Vietnamese to use those books more efficiently. Again, the new series written by him became hot items used in most junior and senior high schools. Eventually he became the first Vietnamese publisher to negotiate for reprint rights in Vietnam of publications originally published by well-known British firms such as Longman & Sons, MacMillan and American firms such as American Book Company and McGraw Hill Book Company.

By the beginning of 1975, Tam's publishing outfit was turning out books in English and Vietnamese by the millions of copies. While he was negotiating for close cooperation with major publishers in Hong Kong, Singapore and Taiwan (Republic of China), the catastrophic event came about in April that same year, forcing him to leave everything behind (especially ESL books)[1] to be later used by the communists.

That past history leaves nostalgic scars with Tam. But what concerned him more than anything after he and his family had to take flight out of communist-ravaged South

---

[1] *ESL: English as a Second Language.*

Vietnam in order to resettle in his new homeland, was how to rebuild his businesses from scratch. His concerns were also similar to those of hundreds of thousands of his compatriots obsessed by such unfortunate circumstances. A long-term transitional phase was soon to begin that required his energies and thoughts to start a new life as he had done three times in his lifetime: the first in 1941 when he got stuck in Hong Kong while the Japanese launched their sneak attack on Pearl Harbor and other strategic bases in the Pacific, the second in 1954 when Vietnam was partitioned along the 17th parallel as a consequence of the Geneva Agreement, and the third in 1975 when South Vietnam was overrun by communist invading forces.

When Tam resettled in Houston, Texas, he already had had over twenty-five years' experience in the publishing business. No Vietnamese ever had any formal training in this line of business, but all of them learned it the hard way. Nevertheless, Tam was confident he was suited to the establishment of a permanent and profitable enterprise. The Vietnamese community in Houston in the summer of 1975 was around 300 people, but currently the unofficial figure shows that there are approximately 50,000 Vietnamese Houstonians!

Tam started his business in a rented two-room apartment unit close to the University of Houston main campus so that he could take up enough courses in the various disciplines.

Being scrupulous, Tam always had an overall long-term plan of what he was to do, and it was specifically scheduled as follows:

- the first stage (3 years: 1975-1978) was primarily geared to have all his ESL text-books reprinted by a small local printing shop.

- the second stage (3 years: 1979-1982) aimed at the reprints of valued cultural publications so as to perpetuate Vietnamese culture (histories, philosophical thoughts, great plays, epic poems, folklores...)

- the third stage (from 1983 to the present) encompasses an ambitious program for systematically turning out bilingual publications in English and Vietnamese of these genres: novels, science fictions, short stories, how-to booklets, guides for small businesses, investments, financing, management, technologies, computer science, medical guides, pamphlets, song books...

If the overseas Vietnamese truly wish to preserve their great traditional culture for the generations to come, they have to be mindful in encouraging the continual publication and use of all literary works. What purpose would it be if they were to teach their children how to read and write Vietnamese if there is to be shortage of supplementary reading materials for the latter? With modern facilities such as word processing appliances, sophisticated printing facilities, audio and video cassettes, computerized retrieval systems... they could easily contribute to this significant cultural preservation for their children and their children's children.

Although the printing facilities in a developed country such as the U.S. are abundant, yet to locate a good and capable printing firm to handle publications in the Vietnamese language was no easy matter in 1975-76. Once the production problem was solved, Tam had to face another tough job, that was, marketing in a new land which was totally unfamiliar to him. There were at that time no Vietnamese-language newspapers or magazines for the promotional campaigns of his new publications.

About one full year after resettling, Tam managed to get in touch with some Oriental foodstores where he placed his products on consignment. And then with extensive advertising in two newly published magazines: "Van Nghe Tien Phong" (Cultural Pioneers) published in Arlington, Virginia, and "Trang Den" (Black and White) published in Glendale, California, his books were selling through retail outlets as described above and through the mail - a phenomenon in this extensive country - that will be discussed in a subsequent passage (p. 167).

Publishing is truly not so simple as it seems, especially in a country like the U.S. where the Vietnamese newcomers are widely scattered over the various regions. The essential point to bear in mind is that the publisher must know his products and market. In order to set up an efficient network, it took Tam almost two full years of diligent and intelligent work while teaching himself the ins and outs of the mail order procedures quite popular in this country. Over a period of time, he built up a list of regular customers who buy their books directly from him. Tam could operate his publishing business in his home and there was no need for a store with fancy shop windows and display-shelves; however, he needed good warehousing to keep the books in impeccable condition.

Tam could usually find books to publish from two prime sources: out-of-print works and manuscripts by experienced and aspiring authors. He was also aware that people are willing to pay higher prices for non-fiction books than for novels, poetry and similar works.

Once he published a book, Tam had the task of selling it to recover his investment. This is a specialized task that every publisher had to be familiar with if he wanted to sell that book himself or he might consider giving it to a sales representative.

In the aftermath of the recessionary years (1982-83) and due to the saturated situation of ESL books and other categories of reprinted Vietnamese books, the market slackened considerably, but Tam is adopting a new policy for his existing operation through a special publicity campaign to promote cultural conservation among the million of overseas Vietnamese. Tam assured his friends that he would continue the publishing business as long as his health permits, for it offers him constant moral satisfaction while it also affords him a modest and decent way of earning his living before retirement.

## B. MAIL ORDER

Thanks to the very efficient U.S. Postal Service that is most beneficial to Tam's publishing business, he could carry out his business from his own residence. The mail order phenomenon is one of the first things he quickly learned through several available materials readily found in most regional and college libraries in his neighborhood. The mail order procedures helped him considerably in his retail sales to the thousands of Vietnamese refugees scattered not only over the United States but also in free countries worldwide.

The U.S. Postal Service, and other parcel delivery agencies such as United Parcel Service (UPS), Purolator Courier, Federal Express.. are exceptionally useful and efficient in semi-wholesale businesses, and finally carriers such as Consolidated Freightways and Central Freight Lines are also specially convenient for his wholesale activities.

Tam's home-based business was indeed small when he started it in Houston, Texas, but it did not take him long to spread the news regarding his re-establishment as a publishing firm to the attention of his fellowmen all over the free world. Orders began to come in through the mail increasingly. Tam was immediately aware that he had to learn the success secrets pioneered by mail order operators. He painted the following reminders on a board hung on the wall just in front of his desk:

- Advertise products for low costs and high returns.
- Keep a sharp watch on costs.
- Satisfy mail order clients to build repeat business.
- Work amicably with the post office.

Tam's business experience instinctively prompted him that mail order selling called for a highly specialized form of marketing. He had to persuade customers whom he never knew and who were hundreds or thousands of miles away from him to place orders with him. Fortunately, Tam was well-known by his fellow-countryfolks for his integrity and credibility over the past thirty years, so they very often sent in their checks or money orders with their purchase orders, and naturally this helped his cash flow significantly.

The mail order business continued to expand as a healthy segment of his publication business and eventually he added cassettes for language study, imported chess games and some FDA approved health care and skin care products.

Tam remarked, after nearly ten years in the mail order business:
- Mail order selling should start small and build with

successful experience.

- Mail order demands a long-pull approach and patience.
- Mail order requires aggressive marketing and very hard work.
- Advertising must be done professionally with an eye to costs and returns.
- Mail order could be profitable, but success depends on marketing the right product and service.

## C. The Cultural Store

Distribution, meaning retail outlets for the products, plays a very important role in the publishing industry. Publications in Vietnamese and bilingually in English-Vietnamese had a strictly limited market in this overwhelmingly English-speaking country. Tam had to negotiate with some Oriental foodstores to place his publications on consignment basis, which they agreed to without too much difficulty, because they also wanted to attract newly arrived Vietnamese residents to their stores. Furthermore during the first year of their arrival, most Vietnamese had to pick up copies of the English-Vietnamese Dictionary and ESL text-books, mostly authored by Tam himself. Consequently, not only Oriental foodstores in Houston but eventually forty-odd stores in the various Vietnam communities, especially those in Orange County (Ca.), Philadelphia (Pa.), Arlington (Va.), New York City (N.Y.), Chicago (Ill.), San Francisco, Los Angeles (Ca.), Denver (Colo.), Dallas (Texas)... accepted Tam's publications on consignment.

But as they increased their food items, rack space for the books became reduced and limited. Since food items were having higher profit margins than books, some of the foodstores were fading out their "books" department, preferring to replace them with meats, seafoods, vegetables and poultry. Furthermore, shoppers when shopping for meat and fish often had soiled fingers and if they browsed through the bookshelves, they would easily spoil the book-covers and inside pages. In the meantime, Vietnamese-language books were being produced in great numbers by several other competitive outfits. Due to those unfavorable reasons, Tam as well as his colleagues realized that it was time for the development and encouragement of Vietnamese specialty stores that deal particularly in books, song sheets, audio and video cassettes, musical instruments, paintings, lacquer pieces, sculptural works, etc.[2] This type of store is now called "cultural store." A friend of Tam's started the first one in Houston, which immediately proved to be very successful. Several other individuals in various Vietnamese communities have also followed the same formula and practically all are faring well.

The publishing business among the Vietnamese communities was heavily affected during the recessionary years (1981-82) and individual businesses slackened considerably. However, thanks to the existence of additional cultural stores, and, hopefully more will open, the Vietnamese publishing houses could survive. Without the well-established and serious-minded publishers overseas to contribute their role in perpetuating Vietnamese culture through publications and other media, the future of Vietnamese culture among the upcoming generations would be left in oblivion. Besides, the Vietnamese authors and writers living in free countries such as the U.S.A., France, England, West Germany, Holland, Switzerland... can continue to express themselves at liberty, while the writers behind the Iron Curtain and Bamboo Curtain are completely under totalitarian control. Wherever and whenever there is no freedom of speech, but only absolute and

[2]*Please read "New Life for Overseas Vietnamese," pp. 74-82.*

blind obedience to dictatorial dogmas, no liberal expressions could become popularized.

The future will justify what true freedom means.

Preservation of a people's culture and heritage is the work of not one single individual but of all those who are concerned with the future of their descendants. The black people in this country are in earnest search for their "roots" as described in style by the great author Alex Haley, the native Indians and Eskimos are also manifesting great efforts in retracing their ancestral cultures. Therefore the Vietnamese immigrants to this "beautiful and spacious land" are responsible in preserving their long-dated culture of fifty centuries. We have to differentiate "citizenship" from "racial origin." The Irish Americans are proud of their ethnic roots; the Jewish Americans, the Japanese Americans... are equally so. Why shouldn't the Vietnamese Americans similarly take pride in their racial grandeur and preserve their culture for ages to come?

## 9. THE TECHNICIANS AND ASSEMBLERS

In a strict sense, these people do not belong to the category of businesspeople, but as they are wage-earners, contributing a considerable and substantial share among the Indochinese newcomers to the numerous new communities, the author feels that it is not out of line to reserve this section in the study to their great efforts since setting foot on the new land.

If the merchant makes his living through trading, that is, the buying and selling of goods in order to generate some profit with which to live on, the great number of Vietnamese blue-collars have traded their hard labor and sweat during these past years to earn their decent living in a country where practically everything was new, strange and unfamiliar to them. The percentage of newcomers still on welfare has decreased significantly during the past three years,[1] and this is evident sign that they are truly eager and anxious to be on their own as soon as circumstances permit.

*The ex-servicemen* from the former Armed Forces of the Republic of Vietnam comprising the enlisted men up to the general ranks came to take refuge in the U.S. in considerable numbers in April, 1975. Most of them spent their entire career in the armed forces during the prolonged Vietnam War (1945-1975) - experiencing exactly thirty years of blood and fire. Their lives were completely dedicated to the national cause and on account of those long years in the armed forces, most of them became professional soldiers without any knowledge of business, technology, or other specific fields. This was their greatest handicap then they came over to this country. Added to this was the language barrier since only a rather small number among those ex-servicemen were fluent in English. It was obvious that with those disadvantages on their side, they

---

[1]*See Tables on pp. 180-187.*

had to double up their willingness and efforts in order to struggle for a living in their new homeland. Just imagine if the American readers were to be similarly handicapped and had to earn their living in a foreign land, and you can easily picture out the situation. How tough it was for those newcomers to hunt for new jobs under extremely awkward situations!

*Patience and Willingness:* Perhaps at no other time was it so trying and challenging to the newcomers than the first year of their resettlement in the U.S. The circumstances simply dictated patience and willingness - the two essential virtues - to the thousands of miserably distressed refugees. Truly, they were patient and willing to start their new lives from scratch in their adopted free country. Not only the ex-servicemen but people of other walks of life also courageously accepted menial work to earn their living, while they would try to learn the English language and some new skills that were being taught in community colleges and continuing education centers whenever they had any "spare" time.

Former teachers, lawyers, architects, physicians, journalists, writers, poets, field officers, even generals... worked hard in positions such as: laundrymen, gas-station helpers, newspaper deliverymen, motel assistants, dishwashers, waiters, kitchen-helpers, wallpaper hangers, construction laborers, signboard painters, social workers, hospital attendants, convenience-store managers, mechanical helpers, probationary draftsmen, apprentice auto-repairmen... All those on-the-job training trades suited the Vietnamese philosophical and stoic temperament, as a Vietnamese maxim says, "The trade teaches itself" (Nghề lại dạy nghề), which can be paraphrased as follows: "If one is willing to learn a new trade by spending his time in apprenticeship, he will eventually learn the trade and can

---

[2]*Ref. "Home Painting," p. 117 and "The Convenience Store Business," p. 154.*

become an expert himself."[2]

The Vietnamese are specially known for their skills in handicraft as they usually show artistic tastes in several lines of crafts such as: silk weaving, lacquer work, silver and gold carving, jade sculptures, embroidery... Though they first learned the arts from the Chinese conquerors, yet as time passed by, they improved on several techniques, sometimes even overpassing their former masters. With the kind of inborn dexterity that most Vietnamese possess, and working under pressure for the upkeep of their families, the diligent and intelligent Vietnamese wage-earners in several respects exerted exceptional efforts to excel and this effectively helped them learn new skills faster than it would normally take.

**The Job Market**

Houston, during the booming years (1976-1980), was typical of the hottest job market for blue collars, because the oil-drilling equipment factories such as Hughes Tools, Cameron Works. Dresser Industries, FMC Corp... were working at full capacity. Responding to such high demand for factory hands, thousands of out-of-state workers were in-migrating to Houston to fill those openings; among them were a great number of Vietnamese factory hands, who were then relatively experienced and had sufficient knowledge of English to get along with their employers as well as their fellow American workers.

**The Female Worker**

In the traditional Vietnamese family, the man is supposed to be the main and only rice-earner, while the primary role of the woman is to maintain good housekeeping and the smoothest harmony among the family members. But when the Vietnamese migrated to the U.S., the American social-economic system has changed the lifestyle in many a Vietnamese family. The high standard of living in the U.S. compels the housewife to take up part-time or full-time job to supplement the family budget. Occasionally she may prove herself to be even more successful than her husband; in several cases, the wives proved to have better English-language ability than their husbands, and the situation may now and then be embarassing in the household.

Quite often for the survival of the family, both husband and wife have to work in earnest. The husband may be a technician in a certain factory, while the wife may apply for a grant to learn some new skills such as hair-styling, key-punching, typing, drafting, nursing and so forth at a professional institute. After having been licensed by the state board, she begins to work full-time so as to bring in additional income to balance the family budget.

While adapting the new American life-style, the Vietnamese woman can depend, in some way, on the assistance of her husband by asking him to share part of the burden of the household chores. With the help of modern electric and electronic appliances, both husband and wife can work out all the house chores on the weekend. If they have teenagers to help, so much the better.

## The Silicon Valley

Currently, in the Silicon Valley (San Jose), the fastest industrial growth is happening in that entire region. One-fifth of this country's 500 fastest-growing companies are in California - more than in any other states. With a gross annual

³Foltz, Kim and Peter McAlley, "Newsweek," March 4, 1985.

product estimated at more than $400 billion, the state now ranks as the No. 8 economic power in the world.[3] The Vietnamese labor force is contributing the second highest percentage in terms of technicians and assemblers to the electronic product factories in that area.

The Vietnamese work force has also made progress not only quantitatively but also qualitatively as shown herebelow:

In the first stage (1976-1979), most of the Vietnamese factory hands only held assemblers' positions, which mean the lowest-paid employees. But by 1980-82, a significant number had risen to the status of technicians and by 1983 to the present time at least 350 have attained the level of engineers in the various factories in the Silicon Valley. This fact also proves a point that while the Vietnamese workers work hard for their living, they also try to improve on their academic background by earning additional college credits aiming at better prospects. It will not be long before hundreds of Vietnamese electrical and electronic engineers will be graduating from technological institutes by the end of this decade.

The common situation is that while the husband works as an engineer or technician in a corporation, his wife or daughter(s) may also work as assemblers in the same firm, with the result that the combined income is usually substantial for a Vietnamese family still maintaining its traditional lifestyle.

Due to the shifting of industrial developments during the past couple of years, the out-migration of Vietnamese residents from Texas to California was 3,433 by June 30, 1983, which added a total of 22,546 migrants to the State of California.[4]

---

[4]*"Refugee Resettlement Program,"* Dept. of Health and Human Services, Washington, D.C. 1984 (Table on p. 70 of this study).

## The Unemployment Problem

Economic growth has given an artificial boost to the unemployment rates, drawing back into the job market many so-called "discouraged" workers, who had given up looking for work and were not counted among the unemployed. What's more, seven million new jobs have been added during this expansion, so more workers are employed now than at any time in the past.

Still, by any standard, unemployment remains high - and for two main reasons. There may not be more so-called "structural unemployment," or joblessness resulting from such sweeping trends as changing technology, demographics or government policy. Moreover, the economy is still not fuctioning at full capacity. Despite the brisk expansion, the 1981-82 recession was so deep that the nation's factories, labor force and many other resources aren't yet being put to their fullest possible use.

"We're not satisfied with 7 percent unemployment... but we accept it," says William Niskanen of the Council of Economic Advisers. "It would be a mistake to target a lower rate of unemployment because it would mean an inflationary monetary policy." Much of America seems to support that view.[5]

Unemployment is almost always considered as a calamity to an area. This fact applies to all the residents without exception. But sometimes, it can be turned into a boon for a certain group of people, who know how to face the situation philosophically with their own planning for the future.

---

[5]Dentzer, Susan and Rich Thomas, "Unemployment: A New Plateau, Newsweek, March 4, 1985.

### The Thirst of Knowledge

When the recession of 1981-82 struck Houston, Texas, a number of Vietnamese laid-offs returned to college to complete their academic study. They received their monthly unemployment checks and when the compensation expired, they began to bite into their savings with a will to complete their undergraduate studies. In June and December 1984, at least 200 Vietnamese students graduated with bachelors degrees in sciences and 50 with masters degrees in the state of Texas, most of whom are now being employed as engineers and specialists in the dozens of major corporations handling defense contracts.

In addition to the young college students who showed extraordinary efforts and willingness to improve on their academic backgrounds, there have also been cases of adults: former teachers and lawyers in Vietnam who recently acquired degrees in electronics and computer science, former military officers and functionaries graduated in engineering and architecture... and are earning their living decently, honestly, and pridefully. Most of the latter are not as fortunate and privileged as those in the medical professions as described on p. 137, but they had to toil and moil exceptionally painfully and bitterly these past ten years. They are indeed living proofs of dignity and patience.

### Demand for Skilled Workers .

Most states want a supply of skilled labor within their borders because this attracts industry. To build their skilled-worker supply, many states lend money to industry for training purposes. Thus, if the entrepreneur has people whose skills he wants to upgrade, he may be in a good position to get a

· hefty loan from his state.

Here is a key wealth-building secret:

"State funds for training can be used for teacher's salaries, teaching aids, and training equipment. Select training equipment that can be used for production - then you will be financed to buy the machines that will make your product."

Many businessmen think of their business in terms of the five Ms of industry:
- Men (by training them)
- Money (through borrowing)
- Markets (the state will help you find them)
- Machines (bought with borrowed money)
- Materials (employees work on while training)[6]

## Learning New Skills

The first decade of the Vietnamese presence in the U.S. has indeed set an era of considerable social-economic changes to the majority of newcomers. From the cases under study the reader must have drawn the conclusions that only a small number of these expatriates could retain their former trades or professions while more than 85% have had to learn new skills or switch to new professions in order to earn their living Writers and poets have become bookkeepers, insurance salesmen, real estate brokers, used car dealers..., housewives are now professional hair-stylists, manicurists, seamstresses, teacher aides, fast-food helpers... and especially, those in the farming business are practically at a complete loss because they are in no way able to compete with American farmers who have been used to mechanical farming procedures. The Vietnamese farmers in this new land have to switch to other

---

[6]*Tyler G. Hicks, "How to Borrow Your Way to a Great Fortune," Parker Publishing Company, West Nyack, N.Y., 1970.*

manual-labor professions for their living: some of them have turned to fishing and shrimping, others have become carpenters, bricklayers, and joined other categories of construction laborers, while a tiny minority have succeeded in growing Vietnamese vegetables and running greenhouses for some particular plants to respond to the demand of their fellow-countryfolks.

The average Vietnamese resettlers are courageous and willing to work even under extreme adversities. They are second to none in terms of stoicism and resignation.

TABLE

Labor Force Participation and Cash Assistance Utilization Rates
Over the First 36 Months of Indochinese Refugee Presence in the US

| | Length of Residence in US (in months) | | | | | | |
|---|---|---|---|---|---|---|---|
| | 0-6 | 7-12 | 13-18 | 19-24 | 25-30 | 31-36 | Over 36 |
| Labor Force Participation (Adults) | 21.6 | 33.3 | 36.6 | 54.6 | 48.9 | 59.0 | 68.4 |
| Percent Receiving Cash Assistance (All Refugees) | 82.7 | 81.7 | 75.6 | 67.3 | 54.0 | 46.3 | 22.7 |

Source: OSI survey data as reported in Office of Refugee Resettlement, Report to the Congress, January 31, 1983, p. 25.

TABLE

Median SSA Earnings of the 1975 Refugees, by 1978-1979 Inter-State Migration Status and Sex, 1978 and 1979

| MOBILITY STATUS | MALES | PERCENT OF MAXIMUM CATEGORY | FEMALES | PERCENT OF MAXIMUM CATEGORY |
|---|---|---|---|---|
| EARNINGS IN 1978, THE YEAR OF THE MOVE | | | | |
| Stayed in CA | $8,201 | 81.1% | $5,543 | 98.4% |
| Stayed in TX | 10,116 | 100.0 | 5,634 | 100.0 |
| Stayed in Other State | 8,843 | 87.4 | 5,234 | 92.9 |
| Moved to CA | 5,736 | 56.7 | 3,523 | 62.5 |
| Moved to TX | 7,000 | 69.2 | 4,112 | 73.0 |
| Moved to Other State | 6,559 | 64.8 | 3,573 | 63.4 |
| EARNINGS IN 1979, THE YEAR AFTER THE MOVE | | | | |
| Stayed in CA | 11,011 | 89.3 | 7,430 | 100.0 |
| Stayed in TX | 12,336 | 100.0 | 7,059 | 95.0 |
| Stayed in Other State | 10,553 | 85.6 | 6,472 | 87.1 |
| Moved to CA | 9,354 | 75.8 | 6,178 | 83.1 |
| Moved to TX | 11,491 | 93.2 | 6,084 | 81.9 |
| Moved to Other State | 9,466 | 76.7 | 5,250 | 70.7 |

Source: SSA Tabulations
Reproduced from: Baker and North, *The 1975 Refugees*, Table 52.

TABLE

Median SSA Earnings of 1975 Refugees, by Sex and State of Residence, 1976 and 1979

| STATE OF RESIDENCE | 1 9 7 6 MALES | | 1 9 7 6 FEMALES | | 1 9 7 9 MALES | | 1 9 7 9 FEMALES | |
|---|---|---|---|---|---|---|---|---|
| | TOTAL | PERCENT OF MAXIMUM CATEGORY | TOTAL | PERCENT OF MAXIMUM CATEGORY | TOTAL | PERCENT OF MAXIMUM CATEGORY | TOTAL | PERCENT OF MAXIMUM CATEGORY |
| Illinois | $5,727 | 100.0% | $2,960 | 91.9% | $9,438 | 100.0% | $5,553 | 98.9% |
| Texas | 5,327 | 93.8 | 2,901 | 90.1 | 9,278 | 98.3 | 5,489 | 97.8 |
| Virginia | 5,110 | 89.2 | 3,220 | 100.0 | 8,000 | 84.8 | 5,348 | 95.2 |
| Other US | 5,039 | 89.2 | 2,698 | 83.8 | 8,489 | 89.9 | 4,860 | 86.6 |
| Pennsylvania | 5,017 | 87.6 | 2,929 | 91.0 | 8,463 | 89.7 | 4,804 | 85.6 |
| New York | 4,886 | 85.3 | 3,148 | 97.8 | 7,518 | 79.7 | 5,615 | 100.0 |
| Florida | 4,852 | 84.7 | 2,720 | 84.5 | 7,539 | 79.9 | 4,892 | 87.1 |
| California | 4,688 | 81.9 | 2,937 | 91.2 | 8,109 | 85.9 | 5,465 | 97.3 |
| Washington | 4,471 | 78.1 | 1,974 | 61.3 | 8,990 | 95.3 | 4,982 | 88.7 |

Source: SSA Tabulations
Reproduced from: Baker and North, *The 1975 Refugees: Their First Five Years in America*, Table 49.

Median OASDHI-Covered Earnings of Selected Groups of 1975 Refugees and All US Workers, 1976-1979

| YEAR | MALE REFUGEES 35-44 | FEMALE REFUGEES 25-34 | ALL REFUGEES | ALL U.S. WORKERS | REFUGEE EARNINGS AS PERCENT OF U.S. EARNINGS |
|---|---|---|---|---|---|
| 1976 | $6,232 | $3,528 | $4,243 | $6,235 | 68.1 |
| 1977 | 7,928 | 4,659 | 5,460 | 6,627 | 82.4 |
| 1978 | 9,863 | 6,159 | 7,053 | 7,148 | 98.7 |
| 1979 | 12,400 | 7,367 | 8,874 | 7,478 | 118.6 |
| Percent Increase 1976-1979* | 98.0 | 108.8 | 109.1 | 19.9 | n/a |

*Unadjusted for inflation.

Sources: Refugee data from SSA tabulations. Data for the US population from Social Security Administration, Social Security Bulletin, Annual Statistical Supplement, 1982, Table 25. The concept used for both groups is median earnings subject to Social Security taxes; average taxable earnings for all US workers were running about $2,000 a year higher in 1979 than shown in this table; average earnings data were not available for the 1975 refugees, but probably were below those of US workers.

Note: The refugee-US earnings comparisons in this table should be viewed against the sex ratios of these two worker populations; whereas in 1979 the refugee worker population was 37.3% female, that of the US work force covered by Social Security was 42.7% female. (The latter percentage was calculated from Table 24 of SSA's Statistical Supplement, 1982.) For more precise age- and sex-specific earnings data, see Table 46.

Reproduced from: Reginald Baker and David North, The 1975 Refugees: Their First Five Years in America (Washington: New TransCentury Foundation, forthcoming), Table 43

TABLE

Median SSA Earnings for Selected Groups of 1975 Refugees, by Sex, 1976 and 1979

|  | 1976 MALES | | 1976 FEMALES | | 1979 MALES | | 1979 FEMALES | |
| VARIABLE | TOTAL | PERCENT OF MAXIMUM CATEGORY | TOTAL | PERCENT OF MAXIMUM CATEGORY | TOTAL | PERCENT OF MAXIMUM CATEGORY | TOTAL | PERCENT OF MAXIMUM CATEGORY |
|---|---|---|---|---|---|---|---|---|
| **STATUS IN INDOCHINA** | | | | | | | | |
| Officer | $5,877 | 100.0% | $3,625 | 100.0% | $12,598 | 100.0% | $7,600 | 94.5% |
| Civil Servant | 5,573 | 94.8 | 3,439 | 94.9 | 11,385 | 90.4 | 8,039 | 100.0 |
| Enlisted | 5,349 | 91.0 | 3,375 | 93.1 | 11,515 | 91.4 | 7,333 | 91.2 |
| Other | 4,270 | 72.7 | 2,899 | 80.0 | 9,265 | 73.5 | 6,808 | 85.2 |
| **OCCUPATION IN INDOCHINA** | | | | | | | | |
| Professional | $5,800 | 100.0% | 3,823 | 100.0% | $12,258 | 100.0% | $8,378 | 100.0% |
| Clerical | 5,114 | 88.2 | 3,773 | 98.7 | 10,972 | 89.5 | 8,011 | 95.6 |
| Manufacturing | 5,327 | 91.8 | 2,850 | 74.5 | 11,429 | 93.2 | 6,626 | 79.1 |
| Construction | 3,992 | 68.8 | 1,620* | 42.4* | 8,902 | 72.6 | 4,250* | 50.7* |
| Service | 5,144 | 88.7 | 2,439 | 63.8 | 10,781 | 88.0 | 6,475 | 77.3 |
| Other | 4,858 | 83.8 | 2,475 | 64.7 | 9,909 | 80.8 | 5,907 | 70.5 |

Source: SSA Tabulations.

* Cells had five and six members, respectively.

TABLE

Median Taxable Earnings of Selected Groups of 1975 Refugees
and U.S. Workers, by Sex
1976-1979

| YEAR | MALES | | | | | | FEMALES | | | | | |
|---|---|---|---|---|---|---|---|---|---|---|---|---|
| | REFUGEES 25-34 | U.S. WORKERS 25-34 | REFUGEES AS % OF U.S. | REFUGEES 35-44 | U.S. WORKERS 35-44 | REFUGEES AS % OF U.S. | REFUGEES 25-34 | U.S. WORKERS 25-34 | REFUGEES AS % OF U.S. | REFUGEES 35-44 | U.S. WORKERS 35-44 | REFUGEES AS % OF U.S. |
| 1976 | 5,560 | 10,519 | 52.9 | 6,232 | 13,427 | 46.4 | 3,528 | 5,098 | 69.2 | 3,216 | 5,154 | 62.4 |
| 1977 | 7,202 | 11,130 | 64.7 | 7,928 | 14,512 | 54.6 | 4,650 | 5,511 | 84.5 | 4,537 | 5,560 | 81.6 |
| 1978 | 9,330 | 12,015 | 77.7 | 9,863 | 15,905 | 62.0 | 6,150 | 6,118 | 100.6 | 6,192 | 6,199 | 99.9 |
| 1979 | 11,707 | 12,501 | 93.6 | 12,400 | 16,750 | 74.0 | 7,367 | 6,497 | 113.4 | 7,674 | 6,629 | 115.8 |

Sources: Refugee data from SSA Tabulations. Data for the U.S. population calculated from Social Security Administration, Social Security Bulletin, Annual Statistical Supplement, 1982, Table 25.

Note: The concept used for both groups is earnings subject to Social Security taxes.

Reproduced from: R. Baker and D. North, The 1975 Refugees: Their First Five Years in America, Table 46

235

TABLE

Monthly Household Income of $800 or More and Individual Weekly Wages
of $200 or More for Different Groups of OSI-Surveyed Refugees, 1975-1980

| SURVEYED POPULATION | WAVE | WHEN CONDUCTED | PERCENT WITH MONTHLY HOUSE- HOLD INCOME OF $800 OR MORE | PERCENT WITH WEEKLY EARNINGS OF OF $200 OR MORE |
|---|---|---|---|---|
| Vietnamese | I | Summer 1975 | 14.9% | n/a |
| " | II | Nov-Dec 1975 | 32.4 | 3.2 |
| " | III | July-Aug 1976 | 41.2 | 5.3 |
| " | IV | Nov-Dec 1976 | 43.8 | n/a |
| " | V | July-Aug 1977 | 51.4 | 14.3 |
| " | VI | Nov-Dec 1978 | 70.0 | 33.7 |
| " | VII | Apr-June 1979 | 75.6 | n/a |
| " | VIII | Oct-Nov 1979 | 79.4 | 49.9 |
| " | IX | Oct-Nov 1980 | 67.6 | 53.7 |
| Cambodian | VI | Nov-Dec 1978 | 63.1 | 29.7 |
| " | VII | Apr-June 1979 | 74.5 | 38.2 |
| " | VIII | Oct-Nov 1979 | 73.8 | 40.7 |
| " | IX | Oct-Nov 1980 | 64.5 | 38.8 |
| Laotian | VII | Apr-June 1979 | 67.4 | 27.9 |
| " | VIII | Oct-Nov 1979 | 59.7 | 36.9 |
| " | IX | Oct-Nov 1980 | 55.8 | 37.1 |

Source: OSI Reports (Generally Tables 13 for earnings, and Tables 15 for income).

TABLE

Distribution of Refugees Filing Income Tax Returns and the Amount of their Adjusted Gross Income and Reported Tax Liability, by Income Level, 1976-1978

| ADJUSTED GROSS INCOME | TAX YEAR 1976 | | | TAX YEAR 1977 | | | TAX YEAR 1978 | | |
|---|---|---|---|---|---|---|---|---|---|
| | TOTAL RETURNS | TOTAL AGI* REPORTED | TOTAL TAX REPORTED | TOTAL RETURNS | TOTAL AGI* REPORTED | TOTAL TAX REPORTED | TOTAL RETURNS | TOTAL AGI* REPORTED | TOTAL TAX REPORTED |
| Less Than $ 5,000 | 12,547 | $32,313,191 | $ 760,308 | 10,428 | $25,419,187 | $ 338,469 | 12,284 | $26,495,728 | $ 336,379 |
| $ 5,000 - $ 9,999 | 8,698 | 60,021,139 | 3,651,657 | 9,823 | 70,332,173 | 4,235,940 | 9,463 | 69,736,206 | 4,501,112 |
| $10,000 - $14,999 | 1,987 | 23,712,419 | 1,828,227 | 3,712 | 44,955,809 | 3,554,050 | 4,960 | 60,353,809 | 5,572,218 |
| $15,000 - $19,999 | 422 | 7,104,821 | 712,786 | 1,394 | 23,736,190 | 2,292,093 | 2,236 | 38,467,732 | 3,388,449 |
| $20,000 - $24,999 | 69 | 1,503,629 | 176,441 | 360 | 7,873,553 | 925,335 | 945 | 20,872,700 | 2,429,787 |
| $25,000 or more | 27 | 798,555 | 132,245 | 123 | 3,737,361 | 593,229 | 428 | 12,675,966 | 1,777,992 |
| TOTAL | 23,750 | $125,454,754 | $7,261,664 | 25,840 | $176,554,273 | $11,939,116 | 30,316 | $228,602,141 | $18,505,937 |
| MEAN** | $5,282 | | | $6,833 | | | $7,299 | | |

*AGI = Adjusted Gross Income

**Derived by dividing "Total AGI Reported" by "Total Returns"

Source: Special printout secured by agreement between Indochinese Refugee Assistance Program, HEW, and the Internal Revenue Service, July 13, 1979.

Taken from Julia Taft, David North, and David Ford, Refugee Resettlement in the U.S.: Time for a New Focus (Washington New Transcentury Foundation, 1979), p. 174.

## 10. THE ORIENTAL FOOD BUSINESS

The typical Chinatown, in San Francisco, New York City, Chicago, Boston, or in any other American city, has alway started with the oriental grocery stores, surrounded by some noodle shops, Chinese restaurants and herbal medicine shops. Similarly, Orange County's "Little Saigon," a mile-long strip of shops and offices, is currently the leading center of Vietnamese life in America that also came into existence with the opening of a couple of oriental grocery stores.

The Orange County chapter of the Vietnamese Chamber of Commerce in America estimates that there are currently (1985) about 650 Vietnamese businesses in Orange County - more than twice the number of Vietnamese businesses in Los Angeles County - generating more than $300 million in sales a year. More than half of the businesses are within four blocks of Bolsa Avenue.[1]

The influx of Indochinese refugees into the United States peaked in 1980 at 167,000 according to the U.S. Office of Refugee Resettlement. By May 1984, an estimated 690,000 Indochinese refugees - about two-thirds from Vietnam, the rest from Laos and Cambodia - had been admitted to the United States. Federal law will limit new refugee arrivals to 50,000 a year in 1984 and 1985, according to the U.S. refugee office.[2]

The above official data is aimed at enabling the reader to have an overall idea of the latest Indochinese population in the U.S., then from those figures realize the significance of the oriental food business on an annual basis.

The author wishes to present only a brief account of the operations of the oriental food business by describing the major

[1]*Day, Kathleen and David Halley, "Vietnamese Create Their Own Saigon," Los Angeles Times.*
[2]*Ibid.*

phases. For over a century since the arrival of the first group of Chinese immigrants in San Francisco who worked as railroad laborers, cooks and laundrymen, the import of Chinese foodstuffs was a specialty business undertaken by a few major Chinese firms with headquarters based primarily in Hong Kong and Singapore. In subsequent years, with the settlement of some contingents of Japanese immigrants in the Los Angeles area, Japanese import-export firms began to be competitive with the Chinese groups.

## IMPORTS

The old-hand, long-established firms owned by Chinese-Americans and Japanese-Americans were having a sort of quasi-monopoly for the imports of oriental food-stuffs in California through the ports of San Francisco and Los Angeles.

What is of concern in this study is the role of Vietnamese and Chinese-Vietnamese who came to settle in the U.S. since the historical exodus of 1975. Particularly, some Chinese-Vietnamese groups, who had had extensive business connections with their counterparts in Hong Kong, Thailand, and Taiwan, were eager to set up business once again in their new homeland quite aggressively. A number of Vietnamese who also had previous knowledge in imports tried to re-establish their enterprises as soon as they settled down in the major cities where the new Vietnamese communities were at their formation stage.

## FINANCIAL BUTTRESS

In spite of great endeavors to re-establish their former businesses in the new land, the Vietnamese as well as the

Chinese-Vietnamese newcomers had to face very keen competition from the long-established import firms which were having exceptionally strong financial support from local and foreign banks. With the financial advantages on their side, these well-anchored entities in many respects were matchless in their rivalry against the new establishments. Furthermore, due to their long years in business experience, and numerous connections in this country as well as their good reputation with suppliers in South East Asia, their credit lines were almost limitless.

## DISTRIBUTION AND RETAIL OUTLETS

For the foodstuff business, marketing, or, in other words, the distribution network plays a very important role that can be considered as a determining factor for the success or failure of the entire enterprise. These retail outlets consist of the hundreds or even thousands of oriental grocery stores spread all over the fifty states wherever there are Asian residents. They owe loyalty, homage and even "gratitude" to their "parent headquarters", which are the main import firms. With such tight network of outlets under their control, the major import enterprises have no dread of minor new competitors who want to take a share of their immense market.

## WAREHOUSING AND INVENTORY

A novice in this line of business might survive for a couple of years if his activities went unnoticed by major corporations. In order to have any success in the oriental foodstuff business, the enterpreneur must be perfectly aware of all the technicalities for warehousing his merchandise. The food items are *perishable* and complex, and have so many characteristics. Without sophisticated knowledge in the storage and maintenance of the thousands of such delicate items, which would deteriorate and spoil quite rapidly, the entrepreneur would soon be faced with serious problems. Let's take a few different lines of foodstuff as examples:

(a).- *Chinese dried mushrooms (tung-koo):* There are dozens of species of "tung-koo," according to the various regions that grow them: North China, Central China, or South China, or even those grown in Japan, Korea, and Taiwan. Then there are numerous sizes, qualities and specific varieties that would give the freshmen a lot of headache. Prices range so extensively while the techniques for storing them also differ according to the various species.

(b).- *Dried shrimps:* There are at least fifty different types of dried shrimps, which require special packing for each type in order to avoid sporadic rodents' attacks. Then, the merchandise itself (dried shrimps) frequently contain bacteria that would gradually spoil the shrimps and turn them into powder form.

(c).- *Sanitary problems:* The manufacturers in South East Asia tried their best to conform to FDA regulations, yet most food items such as rice paper, salted fish, pork sausage, dried squids, fish sauce, dehydrated rice sticks... surely contain microbes and unwanted tiny creatures as detected under the scrutiny of food inspectors.

There are hundreds of other problems concerning warehousing and inventory for this particular line of business. Thus, some new-hands could make reasonable profits at the initial stage, but after a while, they began to realize that all the profits would be eaten up by the remaining spoiled inventory. Very often, when the merchants realized the sad state of matter, the situation would have been too late to be remedied. The end result is that the entire undertaking would go down the drain.

One of the most widely used applications of an operational control system is in the management of a company's inventory. Most companies maintain inventories and, at minimum, calculate actual turnover rates, recognizing the direct relationship between turnover rate, cash flow, and carrying costs. However, the techniques for inventory management go further. Optimum turnover rates can be calculated that balance purchasing or order costs against carrying costs to minimize total expense (figure 1-3). This represents a target - the economic order quantity. Deviations from this target are measurable, both in terms of the operational control system and increased expense. The most productive inventory management operations will be that which comes closest to achieving the optimum turnover rate.[3]

CASH FLOW

The U.S. is one of the few countries that allow absolutely free importation of most kinds of merchandise, especially foodstuffs as long as they conform to FDA regulations. With the powerful U.S. dollar, imported goods are relatively inexpensive and competition has become extremely acute. The consequence is that most major import firms offer extended credit to their outlets (the retailers). This causes the cash flow to slow down considerably, and is another reason for the failure of several smaller and medium-sized import firms which couldn't compete with their larger counterparts.

The major import outfits, as said earlier, usually have strong financial buttress and so they can survive under adverse

[3]*Donald E. Law,, "How to Understand, Monitor, and Control Productivity," Handbook of Business Problem Solving, Kenneth J. Albert, editor in chief, McGraw-Hill Book Company, New York, 1980, p. 8-6.*

circumstances, while the smaller outfits could be facing extremely difficult situations. If the latter do not offer long credit terms to the retailers, they cannot distribute (sell) their merchandise (mostly perishable) within a limited time, but if they allow long credit terms they will have to confront a serious cash flow problem, because the financial institutes would be going after them for repayments while they could not collect from the retailers... This vicious circle often leads the smaller import firms to bankruptcy.

The author has followed the evolution, that is, the booming or blossoming of a number of oriental foodstuff importers as well as their recent withering off, to the astonishment of the local Vietnamese communities who witnessed only the superficial and periodical upsurge of the business while overlooking the great number of shortcomings and errors committed by the interested party.

## THE GROCERY STORES

The capital outlay to open an oriental grocery store may vary from $7,500 to a couple of hundred thousand dollars as it all depends on what size of store an individual wishes to put up and the location of the store. The store-space rental may range from 40 cents per square foot to $1.50 per square foot monthly.
In addition, most oriental grocery stores can negotiate for medium-term credit with the wholesale suppliers: 60 to 120 days, or sometimes even longer, depending on the owner's credit rating.

The following figures are the result of a survey among 100 Vietnamese families during the second semester of 1984 in the Greater Houston area:

## MONTHLY GROCERY EXPENDITURES

An average Vietnamese family consists of 5 members. If we use this figure. for reckoning, we will see that an average Vietnamese or even any other Asian spends about $100 on food per month which can keep him in good health. Thus, if an oriental grocery store is to open in an area which has, say, 500 Asian residents, it can expect a monthly turnover of approximately $25,000 ($50 x 500 = $25,000) with a profit of 15%, equivalent to $3,750 per month, without any debt service to pay off. But if he has to defray any debt service, the net profit may be less. With an income of more or less than $3,000/ month, he and his family can survive, working eight to ten hours a day, six to even seven days a week.

If the Vietnamese residents in his area move in or out the store-owner may expect his income to increase or decrease accordingly. However, should another competitor open a store in his immediate neighborhood, the drastic effect would be felt instantly. Then there is the regrettable situation of price-cutting, unfair competitive strategems, and so on, as some incidents already broke out in oriental shopping centers in Arlington, Virginia, and more underhand artifices could be used if free and unfair competition were allowed to prevail unchecked.

It is a regrettable fact that most people with some capital would like to go into business without the necessary preliminary investigations properly carried out by professional consulting firms as to the feasibility for starting any new business. It is a sort of free-for-all situation that is having full swing in most Vietnamese communities today. The author feels that with a greater number of business failures that will unavoidably come about, the victims will learn and remember their lessons for some time to come. Perhaps, that is the only way to make them aware of the very complex business world in this country. But hopefully, some government or private agencies could come to their assistance before the situation gets worse.

It is very often taken for granted by a great number of people that running a grocery store is so simple and they can survive as long as they work hard. But reality has proven the contrary in numerous cases. Hard work and capital alone cannot bring about success and prosperity to a business. The updated business management knowledge is, in most cases, absolutely required, for the upkeep of the stores. Anyway, if failures are frequent, successes also exist, for there must be someone to cater to the demands of foodstuffs by the hundreds of thousands of Indochinese residents in this country. "The able will survive and prosper, while the unaware will suffer"; that's the rule of business.

*Vegetable growing and local production of several food items:* Please see table on p. 200 and Supplementary Reading p. 243.

## LIVE STOCK BREEDING

The local American supermarkets are filled with countless varieties of foodstuffs at very competitive prices, yet Orientals often find that those readily available items do not respond to their requirements in order to prepare their specialty dishes. Let's consider a couple of typical cases:

Chicken is an inexpensive food item in local supermarkets, but since chickens are almost always bred with feeds containing vitamins and some other chemicals, the taste of such boiled or cooked chicken does not satisfy the oriental gourmets who can easily distinguish that the quality is obviously "under par." So they willingly pay much higher prices to oriental chicken breeders for the right kind of chicken or hen.

For the exquisite "lacquered" roast pork, ducks, and geese, the Oriental, especially the Cantonese, chefs simply must use the oriental-style bred hogs and poultry to turn out those delicacies.

Consequently, in areas where the Asian communities are large in number, live-stock breeding according to traditional and "native" processes is currently developing extensively and profitably. In addition to the Chinese breeders, a number of Vietnamese are now also breeding poultry, hogs, goats, rabbits, frogs, eels, snails, and some species of fish... As long as the demand is brisk, there is someone to take care of the supply!

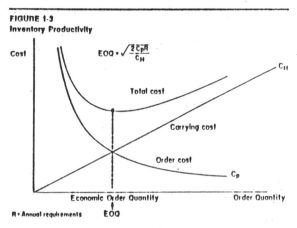

**FIGURE 1-3**
**Inventory Productivity**

Less than optimum performance can be identified with a known relationship to the financial performance of the company. When, for example, a 10 percent reduction in inventory turnover results in a known increase in operating expense, it will also result in a known effect on profits (Figure 1-4). The output/input relationship is clear and measurable, and the responsibility for controlling this expense is assignable. Further, a connection is established between productivity of the inventory management operation and financial performance.

The inventory management example is representative of how the three existing elements in any company can be joined to quantify productivity levels and improvement potential. In this example, the operational system provided the mechanism for identifying optimum performance. It also provided the manager of that responsibility with the method for maintaining day-to-day control. The budget system provided the means for translating an operational performance commitment into the impact of this commitment on the planned financial performance of the company. The accounting system provided the means for converting actual turnover performance into actual

**FIGURE 1-4**
**Costs Based on Turnover**

| Turnover rate | Lot size | Holding cost $\left(\frac{Q}{2} \times C_H\right)$ | + | Order cost $\left(\frac{R}{Q} \times C_p\right)$ | = | Total cost |
|---|---|---|---|---|---|---|
| 16 | 100 | $ 500 | | $8000 | | $8500 |
| 8 | 200 | 1000 | | 4000 | | 5000 |
| 5.33 | 300 | 1500 | | 2670 | | 4170 |
| 4 | 400 | 2000 | | 2000 | | 4000 min. |
| 3.2 | 500 | 2500 | | 1600 | | 4100 |
| 2.67 | 600 | 3000 | | 1330 | | 4330 |
| 2.29 | 700 | 3500 | | 1140 | | 4640 |

$R$ = 1600 units/yr
$C_p$ = $500
$C_H$ = $10

Table      <u>Characteristics of Grocery Stores, 1983</u>

| | Food Cooperatives | Profit-Oriented Stores |
|---|---|---|
| Number | 16 | 12 |
| Average Initial Investment | $20,000 | $32,000 |
| Average Monthly Sales | $ 5,400 | $19,400 |
| Paid Employees[1] | 9 | 12 |
| Clientele – Hmong | 74% | 56% |
|       – Other | 26% | 55% |
| Financial Status – Loss | 21% | –– |
|       – Break Even | 43% | 40% |
|       – Profit | 26% | 60% |

Includes full-time and part-time employees.

(Promotion of Self-Sufficiency Programs among the Hmong, an ethnic tribal group of Vietnam, in the U.S.A.)

Table    Characteristics of Other Small Businesses, 1982-83

| Type of Enterprise | Investors | Initial Investment ($) | Monthly Sales ($) | Paid Employees[9] | Clientele (%) | | Financial Status | | |
|---|---|---|---|---|---|---|---|---|---|
| | | | | | Hmong | Other | Loss | Even | Profit |
| Bakery | 1 | 15,000 | — | 1 | 0 | 100 | | x | |
| Credit Union[1] | — | — | — | 0 | 100 | — | | | x |
| Supermarket/Wholesale Dist.[2] | 11 | 200,000 | 130,000 | 13 | 25 | 75 | x | | |
| Security Guard Service[3] | 3 | 350,000 | 60,000 | 50 | 0 | 100 | | | x |
| Resturant[4] | — | 80,000 | 20,000 | 7 | 0 | 100 | | | x |
| Resturant[4] | 6 | 60,000 | 22,000 | 11 | 0 | 100 | | | x |
| Community Theatre | 2 | 10,000 | 1,500 | 0 | 100 | 0 | | | x |
| Jeweler[5] | 21 | 10,000 | 399 | 1 | 50 | 50 | | x | |
| Wood Crafts[6] | — | 3,000 | — | 2 | — | 100 | | x | |
| Toy Assembly[7] | 1 | 5,000 | 40,000 | 60 | — | 100 | x | | |
| Cleaning Service[8] | — | 2,000 | — | 2 | 100 | 100 | | x | |
| TOTAL (average) | 45 | 736,000 | 274,000 | 147 | (23) | (77) | 2 | 4 | 5 |

Notes:  1. Credit Union has 200 Hmong depositors and functions as non-profit service.
2. Eleven major investors provided initial $140,000. The balance came from 200 small contributors.
3. Two of the investors, providing almost all of the initial capital, were American.
4. The two restaurants belong to the same group of six investors.
5. Operates out of a grocery store.
6. Three hundred members of two Rotary Clubs provided initial support.
7. Operated as sub-contractor in toy factory for six months of 1982.
8. Funded by State as training grant. Venture dormant in mid-1983.
9. Includes full-time and part-time employees.

Table    Characteristics of Farming Projects, 1983

| State | # Families | Acreage | Initial Investment | Initial Investment Per Family ($) |
|---|---|---|---|---|
| Arkansas | 7 | 240 | $ 24,000 | $ 3,400 |
| Arkansas | 10 | 20 | 6,700 | 670 |
| California | 15 | 5 | 9,300 | 620 |
| California | 28 | 32 | --- | --- |
| California | 1 | 45 | 64,000 | --- |
| Iowa | 60 | 15 | 18,000 | 300 |
| Minnesota | 15 | 1,380 | 1,400,000 | 93,000 |
| Minnesota | 3 | 10 | 18,000 | 6,000 |
| Minnesota | 44 | 75 | 16,000 | 360 |
| Minnesota | 35 | 160 | 472,000 | 13,500 |
| Washington | 12 | 22 | 76,700 | 6,400 |
| TOTAL (avg.) | 230 | 2,006 | $2,105,000 | ($10,400)[1] |

[1] The average excluding the project at $93,000/family is about $3,800/family.
(Promotion of Self-Sufficiency Programs among the Hmong, an ethnic tribal group of Vietnam, in the U.S.A.)

Chapter 4

## GENERALIZATION OF THE RESEARCH

- Evaluation and Interpretation

- Perspective and Recommendations

- Suggestions Contributing to Research Methodology

Chapter 4

## GENERALIZATION OF THE RESEARCH

### Evaluation and Interpretation

The ten cases described in the preceding chapter are representative of the entrepreneurial efforts manifested by the Vietnamese newcomers since their first arrival in this country till the present date (April, 1985). The cases depicted the three main categories of business endeavors contributed during the recent first decade of resettlement in the new land.

The author aimed at describing the businesses by grouping them into three categories basing on:

- the traditional trades
- the improved traditional skills
- the newly-learned skills

He attempted to accumulate established knowledge on the selected topic, through research documentations in public and college libraries, the various official departments such as the U.S. Departments of Health and Human Services, Commerce, Education, Housing and Urban Development, Interior, Justice, Labor, as well as numerous other government agencies, services and bureaus. But not much material could be obtained regarding the entrepreneurial activities of the Indochinese new settlers who only came to this country in 1975. At best he could procure from official sources some statistical tables concerning Southeast Asian Refugees Arrivals in the United States (1975 through 1983), their initial resettlement, estimated refugee population by States, secondary migration data, school enrollment of refugee children and so forth, as reproduced in various sections of this study.

Political and military topics concerning the Vietnam War have been published in significant numbers. However, little was available regarding the business activities of the Vietnamese refugees. The author reached the conclusion and decision that he had to organize his own documentation through the following methodology:

(a) Through general observation of some major as well as minor Vietnamese communities which recently came into existence in this country. He would aim his study on the West Coast (San Francisco, San Jose, Orange County, Los Angeles and Seattle) ; on the East Coast (New York City and Arlington, Va.); on the mid-Western area (Chicago and Minneapolis), and on the Southern area (Dallas, Houston and New Orleans). These are the representative localities where large conglomerations of Vietnamese immigrants have set up permanent residence.

(b) The ten representative case studies with their diversified activities could present to the reader a sort of bird's-eye view of the business life among the newcomers during their first ten years of struggle and hard work for survival in their newly adopted homeland. Through the cases described, the reader can have a feeling of scanning over the various entrepreneurial undertakings carried out by the expatriates in the course of this short period of time.

(c) The author attempted to maximize business circles' (meaning Vietnamese in the States) responsiveness to a probing set of questionnaires, but as expected, the number of responses was exceptionally minimal and insignificant to the extent that those responses were not sufficiently valid for any kind of evaluation or conclusion. It was not difficult to understand this negative attitude from the newly-established Vietnamese businesspeople: they did not want "inquisitive outsiders" to know what they were doing, and above all they did not and will not want anyone else to know whether they were successful or unsuccessful. They simply shunned away from any forms of questionnaire!

(d) The most fruitful and valuable results often came from the intimate and casual conversations the author had with hundreds of friends currently scattered in most major Vietnamese communities in this country as well as in Canada, Australia and several European countries thanks to his wide relationship back in Vietnam before the exodus of Spring, 1975. Usually, in those conversations and with the counterparts' permission to use a handy portable taperecorder, he could gather very useful and down-to-earth information relevant to the progress and development or the failures in the various lines of business. Exchange of viewpoints in such circumstances often lead to interesting new ideas that could contribute to the improvement of business enterprises undertaken by the overseas Vietnamese.

(e) Telephone contacts with friends all over the States, asking them pertinent questions as to their business development and expansion, were often successful in obtaining substantial feedbacks.

(f) The author's personal visitations to his business acquaintances in the various metropolitan areas where there are Vietnamese "towns" such as Westminster (Orange County), Garden Grove, Dallas, Houston, Arlington...

constitute the best approach to gather information and also to have first-hand observations on the progress and changes that have been going on.

(g) Personal correspondence to friends and acquaintances' all over the U.S. as well as in other places with specific requests to them to feed back with whatever they have observed in their respective communities, has helped in contributing very practical and objective remarks to the overall documentation on the living conditions, especially on the business life of the Vietnamese expatriates since 1975.

**Perspectives and Recommendations**

(a) The limited market versus the general market:  By reading through the ten typical cases as presented in the preceding chapter, the reader can easily draw the following general conclusions:

- the "limited market" signifies the market that aims at the Vietnamese residents who usually consist of only .3%, or even less, of the entire population of a certain area. So, out of one thousand residents only three are Vietnamese.  The consequence is that the point of saturation will be reached very soon and once competition becomes keen, the percentage of business failures will also increase rapidly.

- the "general market" responds to the demands of *all* the residents in an area, and consequently the chance for success and expansion is greater.

On account of this primordial reason, the Vietnamese expatriates should bear this reality in mind when doing business in a "foreign" country.  They should in several respects imitate their Italian, Mexican, Greek, German counterparts and be more pragmatic and open-minded as far as business undertakings are concerned.

(b) Money management: Perhaps the main worry for any businessperson is money, for without it no business can be started. No one can deny the fact that money worries have been the causes of "the mistakes, the tension, the restrictions of the spirit and damage to human dignity."[1] So, the first essential thing for the starting enterpreneur to learn is: "The key fact, the ultimate secret is this: Nearly every person who built wealth for himself in recent years did so on borrowed money - that is, he started with little or no money and wound up with a lot of money!"[2]

The businessman in a capitalist country like the U.S.A. must know at least how to apply to his business the basic valuable financial principles, which normally include: "true and apparent interest rates, loan pay off time, refinancing..."[3] He should have in hand a good book of business arithmetic and review the many short-cuts he could use to compute interest costs, installment payments, note and draft discounts, mortgage and down payments.[4]

In addition, the businessperson must be familiar with:

- the essential tools in financial management.
- raising money (capital)
- tax traps and opportunities
- inventory management
- crisis management

(c) A must for all businesspeople, especially for the Vietnamese newcomers doing business in this new land, is to

[1]Price E. Patton, "Free from Money Worries," (preface) Bantam Books, Chicago, Ill. 1956, p. 1.
[2]Tyler G. Hicks, "How to Borrow Your Way to a Great Fortune," Parker Publishing Co., West Nyack, N.Y., 1970, p. 17.
[3]"Free From Money Worries."
[4]R.R. Rosenberg and Harris Lewis, "Essentials of Business Arithmetic." McGraw Hill, New York, 1964.

know how to *save, invest* and *insure.*

"Unless the businessperson has other cash available, he must *save.* How and where he saves will depend upon the amount which can be set aside at one time."[5]

If he can invest some of his money, he has to follow this advice: "Never put all your eggs in one basket unless you can sit by and watch them hatch." He should consider buying a piece of real estate only when he has accumulated sufficient resources.[6] Too many Vietnamese bought up real estate when in reality they were not yet well equipped financially. The depression of 1981-83 caused many a family to lose their properties.

The businessman should also read and learn more about insurance which is such a complex subject itself, and without which, no one could feel safe and comfortable in carrying on his business in this country

(d) Raising money

So far almost 95% of the overseas Vietnamese businesspeople are using whatever capital they have on hand, especially through savings, to start their businesses. This is in fact considered to be the classical and conservative way to initiate a business, and this outmoded practice is also the greatest shortcoming among them while they do not know how to use the facilities that financial institutes and government agencies are offering them.

The author wishes to recommend the following to current and potential Vietnamese entrepreneurs to focus their attention on the following hints for their benefits in the development and expansion of their businesses:

"Money to make money - that's the role capital plays in your business. Money or an equivalent, such as "sweat equity," can come from many sources. Sometimes, to avoid undercapitalization, you tap them all. You learn how to:

- Figure how much money you need.
- Develop a plan to acquire the money you need.
- Use SEM (Somebody Else's Money) to finance part of your business.
- Call on the Small Business Administration for help.
- Discover little-known sources for venture capital.
- Apply substitutes to reduce capital needs.
- Play the "little bit from many" game to borrow funds."[7]

(e) Which organization is best?

Basically, there are only three choices:

- Proprietorship: An individual simply owns the business.

- Partnership: Two or more people own the business.

There are two kinds of partnership: a general partnership and a limited partnership.

- Corporation: A number of individuals form a legal "person" authorized by the state to operate like an individual. Corporations exist only when chartered by a state.

The businessperson should ask the advice of a lawyer as to these six points before selecting the form of organization best for him:

[7]Merle E. Dowd, "How to Earn a Fortune and Become Independent in Your Own Business," Parker Publishing Co., West Nyack, N.Y., 1971, p. 177.

- Costs and difficulty
- Control of risks
- Continuity and longevity
- Administration flexibility and control
- Effects of laws on business organizations
- Ability to attract capital.[8]

(f) Franchising

One business phenomenon that the Vietnamese entrepreneurs began to hear of more and more frequently in the U.S. is franchising. At first he might not pay any attention to this new terminology, but like any other newcomers to this country, he cannot escape that word as it strikes his ears again and again until he has to ask his American friends what franchising is all about. Sometimes he may get the proper explanation, but most of the time he may get wrong answers to his query.

The best bet is to *read a lot about this subject matter* and then come to an SBA office and ask some qualified person to explain it as clearly as possible, using concrete examples to illustrate the various phases of franchising.

Anyway, from statistics it has been proven that the odds of success in franchising is as much as eight to one compared to a business started on an individual basis. New franchises pop up every day, it seems. One of them could be the newcomer's ticket to a business of his own. Currently more than 850,000 franchises are operating, and new ones are joining the field at a rate of 40,000 per year.[9]

"The franchise has become the great American dream for people eager to be his own boss. But the prospective

---

[9]*"How to Earn a Fortune...," p. 148.*

entrepreneur must remember that buying a franchise for a restaurant, 'car repair or other national chain is *not always* a ticket to financial success or even career independence," said Stan Luxenberg, author of "Roadside Empires - How the Chains Franchised America," published by Viking. He also warned, "Most new businesses fail and most chains' franchises fail."

So, here again, the prospective entrepreneur must be extremely cautious when getting into any business whether on an individual basis or on the franchising formula. He must be on the watch-out, for a false step and a poor decision may cost him his whole fortune.

(g) *Main causes of failures among Vietnamese entrepreneurs:*

According to information publicized recently by the Los Angeles Chamber of Commerce, the following were the key factors leading to most of the business failures among the Vietnamese new entrepreneurs:

- Lack of professional experience and know how.
- Neglecting to follow proper instructions.
- No strong will power to accept hard work.
- No willingness to adapt themselves to new circumstances and conditions.
- Using their available funds in unnecessary items.
- Shortage of capital to take over good businesses when opportunities present themselves.
- Insufficient capital to buy up good merchandise at fair prices.
- No marketing survey.
- Inability in management such as: inventory control,

personnel management, financing, taxes...
- Competition has become too acute.
- Started businesses now considered obsolete.

The foregoing is only a condensed form of presenting the current shortcomings confronted by the Vietnamese newcomers. If no appropriate solutions are brought up in the months and years to come, the situation will certainly deteriorate to the extent that a significant number of Vietnamese entrepreneurs will be forced into a "gloom and bust" dead-end.

### (h) *Managerial and Operative Functions*

In analyzing the ten representative cases presented in chapter 3 of this study, the reader must have formed an opinion on the factors leading to some successes and some failures with the latter in a prevailing position. The main cause for most failures or potential failures among the Vietnamese businesspeople is the lack of modern business management knowledge - not necessarily the sophisticated advanced levels, but the basic knowledge that any small businessperson should possess before getting involved in this line of activity.

A business organization is composed of people who "work" together.[10] Since a leader or manager is always a member of an organization, it follows that his work is called "managerial." Those people whom he leads perform the "operative" work. Thus we have a twofold classification of work: managerial and operative.[11] And we can classify functions (work) as two kinds: managerial functions and operative functions. Managerial functions are those involving leadership. Operative functions are those directly concerned with producing or selling goods or services.[12]

---

[10]*Robert D. Hay, "Introduction to Business," Holt, Rinetrart and Winston, Inc., New York, 1968, p. 23.*
   [11]*Ibid., p. 23.*
   [12]*Ibid., p. 23.*

Consequently, in order to attain some degree of success in business in a country where free enterprise is in full bloom, which means that free and fair competition is also encouraged, an average businessperson must have at least the fundamental knowledge of management, which is itself "the art and science of achieving goals through people and other resources."[13]

If a case of failure should come to the entrepreneur's attention, it is suggested that he should make an immediate analysis of the factors that lead to that undesirable consequence. He should scrutinize on causes such as: general description of the enterprise so as to form an overall image of it, the performance, the top level management, who makes policy and decisions, how good ethics were being performed, the personnel situation, the objectives of the firm, what kind of planning did it have, how was the acquisition function, the inventory, what was the overall organizing system, how was the actuating function, how about the performance of the evaluating or control function, any additional concluding thought, and finally an examination of the estimated balance sheet.

A rapid analysis based on the above suggested hints can be very helpful in pinpointing the strong and we..k points of an average enterprise.

According to a press release published on the "Vietnam Time", March 1984 issue, the following information was made known to the Vietnamese entrepreneurs on the East Coast:

## PILOT BILINGUAL TRAINING FOR VIETNAMESE ENTREPRENEURS by GEORGETOWN UNIVERSITY GOT A GOOD START

Washington, D.C. (VNT) — The first pilot bilingual

---

[13]*Ibid.*, p. 37.

training program for Vietnamese entrepreneurs in the Washington area, by Georgetown University, got a pretty good start, according to director of the program, Prof. Pho Ba Long, formerly a dean of Dalat University in South Vietnam.

The program proposes to increase the chance of success of the Vietnamese entrepreneurs within the American business environment. It is funded by the Center for Immigration Policy and Refugee Assistance (CIPRA) of Georgetown University, a prestigious U.S. Catholic Institution in Washington D.C. As many as 25 scholarships are designated to be granted to eligible applicants.

The instruction, as planned, has been given bilingually in Vietnamese and English. The training has been carried out in the form of lectures and group discussion.

Another project that can be of great assistance to the newcomers who run small businesses in the U.S. is:

National Refugee Rights Project

The San Francisco Lawyers' Committee for Urban Affairs has received a $50,000 grant from the Ford Foundation to establish a National Refugee Rights Project.

For the past three years, the Lawyers' Committee has sponsored the Bay Area Immigrant and Refugee Rights Project. The Ford grant will allow the Committee to add a national component to its policy impact efforts on behalf of the refugee community.

"The National Project will focus on federal policies and practices that restrict refugees' access to public benefits and inhibit their ability to attain economic self-sufficiency," said Robert Rubin, Managing Attorney of the Immigrant and Refugee Rights Project. The Bay Area project already has achieved major victories such as restoring $5.2 million in cash and medical benefits to refugees as well as successfully challenging a state law that restricted refugees access to state colleges.

As in all Lawyers' Committee endeavors, the National Project will rely heavily on the pro bono support of the private bar. When national issues develop outside the Bay Area, the Project will call on local Lawyers' Committee affiliates elsewhere as well as other legal services, organizations, and local bar associations to assist in attracting pro bono counsel.

The National Refugee Rights Project will utilize class action litigation and other advocacy activities in its challenges to federal policies that not only adversely affect refugees during the initial resettlement period but frustrate their subsequent efforts to receive adequate medical care, secure gainful employment, pursue higher education or obtain critically needed public benefits.

"No other legal advocacy organization in the country focuses exclusively on the legal entitlements of refugees," said Rubin. "It has been our experience that because the refugee community has not had significant access to lawyers who are willing to bring major challenges against legally suspect policies and practices, the likelihood of success in pursuing a legal strategy at this time is strong.

For further information, contact: Robert Rubin, Managing Attorney, Immigrant and Refugee Rights Project, 625 Market St., Suite 915, San Francisco, CA. 94105 - Tel: (415) 543-9444.

*Suggestions contributing to research methodology*

At the time of writing this study, as already mentioned previously, documentation concerning the business enterprises undertaken by Vietnamese immigrants in the U.S.A. during the first decade (1975-1985) was extremely scarce. However, from recent information, it has been learned that chambers of commerce have come into existence at the initiative of Vietnamese entrepreneurs in areas such as Orange County, Los Angeles, San Francisco, Houston, Arlington and so forth. In addition, U.S. Government and regional departments, agencies and bureaus are now compiling statistics, records, reports, and numerous other documentations relevant to the economic, financial, industrial, cultural and social activities and contributions of the Vietnamese-Americans in this country.

The author feels optimistically assured that by 1990 - that is five years hence - ample materials will be readily available in the various libraries and archives. Furthermore, by that time, undoubtedly more research studies and publications on this subject matter will also be compiled by individuals and private societies that have special interests in the evolutionary developments of the Vietnamese ethnic group in the U.S.A.

In later years, when funds are available and when the Vietnamese entrepreneurs begin to realize the importance of furnishing useful data to build up reliable information centers, questionnaires and other forms of data-gathering procedures could be prepared by individual researchers or professional agencies to be sent out to the thousands of Vietnamese-run businesses, for useful feedbacks, which are essential to future elaborate studies.

This modest paper serves only as an initial stepping stone on the long research road leading to sophisticated studies on the Vietnamese cultural and economic contributions to this nation of Freedom and Justice. The author hopes that his humble efforts will bring about encouragement to his compatriots and also to induce other writers and scholars to contribute further to the subject matter.

Chapter 5

## CONCLUSIVE REMARKS

- Recommended Reading

- Organizations Helpful to Entrepreneurs

Chapter 5

## CONCLUSIVE REMARKS

The results of the author's study, directed towards the determination of the great efforts manifested, during the past decade, by the Vietnamese refugee-immigrants to the U.S.A., the delineation of the successes and failures among the Vietnamese entrepreneurs, and the elaboration on the true meaning of the free enterprise system as carried out in a democratic and capitalistic nation, hopefully can contribute in some way to future more detailed and profound researches on business developments among the various Vietnamese communities in this country and elsewhere.

The Vietnamese Americans, like their other ethnic minority brothers, came to this land as refugees or immigrants in search of freedom and justice. Some have been fortunate to be able to adapt themselves to the new mode of life without encountering major psychological and physical impacts, while not a small number have experienced extreme difficulties in several aspects. Some have had no problems in getting along in the American mainstream of life, and these are the few fortunate individuals, while the majority have had to face so many daily frustrations in all walks of life.

In general, every day the newcomers witness the high standard of living enjoyed by American citizens and must admit that this standard of living shows signs of becoming higher and higher as the years go by. The materialistic criteria of the people in the U.S.A are undeniably more desirable than any criteria established in the socialist or communistic bloc. Marxist sociology, which is an economic doctrine, is just simply being outdated in this modernistic world. It might have been successful in luring some individuals into its old teachings and dogmas in the late 19th century or early 20th century, when the social and economic conditions of the laboreres and farmers were deplorable, but since the aftermath of World War II, the Marxist philosophy has entered its declining stage with some followers only from backward, former colonialized, and underdeveloped nations. The 80's mark the beginning of the ending phase of Marxism-Leninism.

"There are two major reasons for the American's high standard of living. One is their system of economic freedom which allows them to produce and sell goods and services. The second is the efficiency of the business organizations, working in the economic system of freedom, which actually produce and sell the goods and services that are a part of the Gross National Product (GNP).

The key word to the American system is economic freedom. America was founded as a country because of the belief that men are free, under God, to enjoy life, liberty, and the pursuit of happiness. The pursuit of happiness is encouraged by allowing men to enjoy certain freedoms."[1]

For every economic freedom that society grants it requires a corresponding obligation. Economic freedom is a two-sided coin. One side involves freedom and the other side an obligation to perform some useful service.[2]

Thus, while the Vietnamese expatriates have chosen this country to be their adopted homeland like millions of their predecessors of numerous ethnic stocks, they ought to resolve

[1]Robert D. Hay, "Introduction to Business," Holt, Rinehart and Winston, New York, 1968, p. 4.
[2]Ibid., p. 5

in respecting the "following freedoms while contributing to the improvement of the standards of living:

1.- Consumer sovereignty
2.- Private property
3.- Freedom of choice
4.- Personal incentives
5.- Freedom to compete
6.- Freedom from undue governmental interference"[3]

These characteristics contribute to an economic free enterprise system which in turn contributes to a higher standard of living - a goal that all freedom-loving people aim for.

The vaunted "worker's paradise" which communism was supposed to bring to the people living under the totalitarian rules falls far short of its promise. Facts regarding the living standards of the people of Eastern Europe, Cuba, Vietnam, Ethiopia, Nicaragua... hardly reflect the picture presented to developing countries either by communism or socialism.

---

[3]*Ibid., p. 8.*

# RECOMMENDED READING TO THE VIETNAMESE ENTREPRENEURS DOING BUSINESS IN THE U.S.A.

- The "Management Workbooks for Self-Employed People" Series comprising five volumes: The Business Review, The Business Plan, Basic Finance, Basic Marketing, Managing Time & Personnel - published by Dodd-Blair & Associates, P.O. Box 644, Maine 04970.

- The American Entrepreneurs' Association (AEA) Business Manuals published by the AEA, 631 Wilshire Blvd., Santa Monica, CA. 90401

- James A. O'Brien, "Computers in Business Management," (3rd Ed.), Richard D. Irwin, Inc., Homewood, Ill., 1982.

- "Small Business Reporter" - a publication issued ten times a year by the Bank of America, San Francisco, CA. 94120.

- Joseph L. Massie, "Essentials of Management," Prentice-Hall, Englewood Cliffs, New Jersey, 1971.

- Bernard Greisman, editor, "How to Run a Small Business," J.K. Lasser Tax Institute, McGraw-Hill Book Company, New York, 1982.

- "Key Business Ratios and Cost of Doing Business" are statistical data sources issued free by Dun & Bradstreet Inc., 99 Church St., N.Y., N.Y. 10007.

- Merle E. Dowd, "How to Earn a Fortune and Become Independent in Your Own Business," Parker Publishing Co., Inc., West Nyack, N.Y. 10994.

- "Tax Guide for Small Business," IRS publication No. 334 is issued yearly.

- Small business management series - aimed at improving managerial capabilities. Useful titles include:

Sales Training for the Smaller Manufacturer
The Foreman in Small Industry
A Handbook of Small Business Finance
Insurance and Risk Management for Small Businesses
and several others.

- Starting and managing series include:

Starting and Managing a Service Station
Handbook on Small Business (5th ed.) 228 pages, $7.00 per copy.

- Business research series include:

The First Two Years: Problems of Small Firm Growth and Survival

- Booklets that provide specialized information:

Effort Marketing for Smaller Firms
Managing for Profits

- SBA publications may be ordered from the Superintendent of Documents, U.S. Government Printing Office, Washington D.C. 20402.

- Many government programs can aid small business. For a list of Free and Low-Cost Government Services for Small

Business, send $1 and a stamped, self-addressed envelope to Mark Stevens, P.O. Box 487, Chappaqua, N.Y. 10514.

- W. Jack Duncan, "Essentials of Management," The Dryden Press, Hinsdale, Illinois, 1975.

- John P. Kotter, "The General Managers," Harvard Business Series, The Free Press, a division of Macmillan Publishing Co., New York, 1982.

- David L. Markstein, "Money Raising and Planning for the Small Business," Henry Regnery Co., Chicago, Ill., 1974.

- Vernon A. Musselman & Eugene H. Hughes, "Introduction to Modern Business," 5th ed., Prentice-Hall, Englewood Cliffs. N.J. 1968

touch with some Oriental foodstores where he placed his products on consignment. And then with extensive

McGraw-Hill Book Co., New York, 1968.
- Howard J. Ruff, "How to Prosper During The Coming Bad Years," Warner Books, Inc., New York, 1980.
- Irving J. Shapiro, "Dictionary of Marketing Terms," 4th ed., Totowa, N.J., Littlefield, Adams & Co., 1981.

- A. Edward Spitz, "Marketing Resources: Allocation and Optimization," Petrocelli Books, New York, 1974.

## ORGANIZATIONS THAT CAN BE HELPFUL
## TO NEW SMALL ENTREPRENEURS

- AMERICAN BAR ASSOCIATION
  American Bar Center, 3460 Wilshire Blvd.
  Los Angeles, CA. 90010, (213) 387-7375

- ASSOCIATED CREDIT BUREAUS
  P.O. Box 218300, Houston, Texas 77218
  (713) 492-8155
  For complaints about credit bureaus.

- COALITION FOR THE PROTECTION OF
  VIETNAMESE BOAT REFUGEES
  c/o IRAC
  1424 16th Street NW, Suite 404
  Washington D.C., 20036

- GULF COAST SMALL BUSINESS DEVELOPMENT
  CENTER (GCSBDC) HOUSTON CENTER
  101 Main Street, Houston, Texas 77002
  This center will help out small business in 40 surrounding
  counties.

- INDOCHINESE RESOURCE ACTION CENTER (IRAC)
  1424 16th St. NW, Suite 404
  Washington, D.C. 20036

- INTERNATIONAL FRANCHISE ASSOCIATION
  1025 Connecticut Ave., N.W.
  Washington D.C. 20036 - (202) 659-0790

- MINORITY BUSINESS DEVELOPMENT CENTER
  There are about 100 such centers all over the country, in·

particular, California has the following:

- Los Angeles MBDC: 3460 Wilshire Blvd., 1006-7
  Los Angeles, CA. 90010. (213) 382-5032

- San Diego MBDC: 6363 Alvarado Court, 225
  San Diego, CA. 92120. (619) 265-3684.

- Sacramento: Price Waterhouse, 455 Capitol Mall
  Sacramento, CA. 95814. (916) 441-2370

- Stockton: Price Waterhouse, 2291 West March Lane
  #227D
  Stockton, CA. 95207. (209) 474-3553.

Export Development Program:

- Development Associates, San Francisco (415) 776-0120
- Cardinal Management, Los Angeles, (213) 385-1335
- Development Consultant, San Diego State University, San Diego, CA. Phone (619) 286-5623

Rural Assistance Program

- Development Associates, San Francisco, (415) 776-0120

Minority Trade Association Program

- MBDA Private Sector Program Division (202) 377-3277
- The National Minority Supplier Development Council, 1412 Broadway, 11th Floor, New York, NY. 10018. Phone (212) 944-2430.

Information Clearing House

- MBDS US Department of Commerce, Washington, D.C. 20230. Phone (202) 377-2648.

- MINORITY SERVICE GROUP, INC.
  2323 Voss, Suite 650
  Houston, Texas 77057. (713) 975-0313

- NATIONAL CENTER FOR FINANCIAL EDUCATION
  2107 Van Ness Ave., San Francisco, CA. 94109
  Phone: (415) 474-8496

- OFFICE OF REFUGEE RESETTLEMENT
  Dept. of Health and Human Services
  Washington D.C. 20201

- SCORE Counselors: Service Corps of Retired Executives (SCORE) includes experienced men and women who volunteer their services to help small businesspeople with operating problems. They serve *without pay.*

- Small Business Administration (SBA): Personal counseling on many business problems is available at the 78 field offices of the SBA located in principal cities in the U.S.

- SMALL BUSINESS ADMINISTRATION
  1441 L. St., N.W., Washington D.C. 20416
  SBA Answer Desk: (800) 368-5855

- SMALL BUSINESS MANAGEMENT TRAINING:
  Georgetown University's Center for Immigration Policy and Refugee Assistance (CIPRA), in conjunction with the School for Summer and Continuing Education, is sponsoring a 12-week pilot training program in small business management for Vietnamese refugees and immigrants. The

training is offered as a part of the Small Business Development Center's program at Howard University, with which Georgetown has recently become affiliated. Courses and seminars are scheduled to start in the near future and will be conducted bilingually in Vietnamese and English. For details call CIPRA at (202) 625-3545.

- STATE AIDS: Most states offer some form of financial assistance or advice to small businesses. Contact SBA field office for leads to such assistance or write to the Regional Development Laboratory, 4040 Locust St., Philadephia, PA. 19104.

- U.S. DEPARTMENT OF COMMERCE
  Andrew Kostecka, Franchise Specialist, Room 4312
  Washington D.C. 20230. (202) 377-0342.

# APPENDIX A

# Southeast Asian Refugee Populations in the U.S.

## (By State of Residence - As of 1/31/85)

| State of Residence | Estimated Total | State of Residence | Estimated Total |
|---|---|---|---|
| Alabama | 2,700 | Nevada | 1,900 |
| Alaska | 200 | New Hampshire | 700 |
| Arizona | 4,700 | New Jersey | 6,400 |
| Arkansas | 2,400 | New Mexico | 1,900 |
| California | 290,200 | New York | 25,500 |
| Colorado | 10,800 | North Carolina | 5,200 |
| Connecticut | 6,800 | North Dakota | 900 |
| Delaware | 300 | Ohio | 9,900 |
| District of Columbia | 1,400 | Oklahoma | 8,400 |
| Florida | 11,800 | Oregon | 17,400 |
| Georgia | 8,600 | Pennsylvania | 24,300 |
| Hawaii | 6,400 | Rhode Island | 5,300 |
| Idaho | 1,400 | South Carolina | 2,100 |
| Illinois | 24,000 | South Dakota | 900 |
| Indiana | 3,900 | Tennessee | 4,700 |
| Iowa | 8,500 | Texas | 52,500 |
| Kansas | 9,700 | Utah | 8,100 |
| Kentucky | 2,000 | Vermont | 600 |
| Louisiana | 13,800 | Virginia | 21,400 |
| Maine | 1,600 | Washington | 33,300 |
| Maryland | 8,700 | West Virginia | 400 |
| Massachusetts | 20,100 | Wisconsin | 10,500 |
| Michigan | 10,100 | Wyoming | 200 |
| Minnesota | 23,000 | Guam | 200 |
| Mississippi | 1,700 | Other Territories | * |
| Missouri | 6,400 | | |
| Montana | 800 | *Fewer than 100 | |
| Nebraska | 2,000 | | |
| | | **TOTAL** | 726,700 |

*Source:* Office of Refugee Resettlement

# Southeast Asian Refugee Arrivals in the U.S. and Third Countries

## (April 1975 through January 1985)

| Country of Residence | Estimated Total | Country of Residence | Estimated Total |
|---|---|---|---|
| Australia | 97,592 | Japan | 1,159 |
| Belgium | 6,568 | Netherlands | 5,933 |
| Canada | 111,746 | New Zealand | 6,378 |
| China | 265,775 | Norway | 5,033 |
| Denmark | 3,497 | Sweden | 3,961 |
| France | 107,307 | Switzerland | 9,858 |
| W. Germany | 28,513 | United Kingdom | 18,815 |
| Italy | 3,486 | Other | 23,024 |

| | |
|---|---|
| Total in the U.S. | 731,216 |
| Total in Third Countries | 698,618 |
| GRAND TOTAL | 1,429,894 |

*Source:* Department of State

## Geographic Location and Movement

Southeast Asian refugees live in every State and several territories of the United States. Large residential concentrations can be found in a number of West Coast cities and in Texas, as well as in several East Coast and Midwestern cities. Migration to California continued to affect refugee distribution during FY 1983, but at the same time several Eastern States experienced significant growth due to both secondary migration and initial placement of refugees.

Because the INS Alien registration of January 1981 was the most recent complete enumeration of the resident refugee population, it was the starting point for the current estimate of their geographic distribution. (These 1981 data appeared in the ORR report to the Congress for FY 1982.) The baseline figures as of January 1981 were increased by the known resettlements of new refugees between January 1981 and September 1983, and the resulting totals were adjusted for secondary migration, using new data discussed below. The estimates of the geographic distribution of the Southeast Asian refugee population derived in this manner are presented in Table 9.

At the close of FY 1983, the fourteen States with the largest estimated concentrations of Southeast Asian refugees were:

| State: | Number: | Percent: |
| --- | --- | --- |
| California | 244,100 | 37.1% |
| Texas | 53,600 | 8.1% |
| Washington | 30,400 | 4.6% |
| Illinois | 23,500 | 3.6% |
| Pennsylvania | 23,000 | 3.5% |
| New York | 22,700 | 3.4% |
| Minnesota | 21,000 | 3.2% |
| Virginia | 20,300 | 3.1% |
| Oregon | 16,200 | 2.5% |
| Massachusetts | 15,400 | 2.3% |
| Louisiana | 13,300 | 2.0% |
| Florida | 11,700 | 1.8% |
| Colorado | 10,100 | 1.5% |
| Michigan | 10,000 | 1.5% |
| TOTAL: | 515,300 | 78.2% |
| Other: | 143,700 | 21.8% |
| TOTAL: | 659,000 | 100.0% |

These fourteen States were also the top fourteen States in terms of Southeast Asian population one year previously, at the close of FY 1982. California, Texas, and Washington have held the top three positions since 1980. Only minor changes took place in the rank order of these fourteen States during FY 1983. After the top three States, the next five are within a few thousand of each other, so their relative rank means less than it did in previous years. The proportion of Southeast Asian refugees living in California is now estimated at 37.1 percent, an increase from the estimated 36.4 percent of one year earlier. Again this growth occurred through secondary migration, since Califonia received a lower share of initial placements in FY 1983 than its share of the total population. Four other States on this list are estimated to have grown both in absolute numbers and in their proportion of the refugee population: Illinois, New Work, Massachusetts, and Florida. [1]

[1]*Report to the Congress, Jan. 31, 1984, Refugee Resettlement Program, U.S. Department of Health and Human Services.*

# APPENDIX B

# SUPPLEMENTARY READING MATERIALS

# CHẢ GIÒ[1]
## The Egg-Roll

*Ed's Note.— Like the hamburger, to Americans, the fish-and-chip to the British, the paté chaud to the French, the pizza to Italians, the taco to Hispanics, and the egg-rolls to the Chinese, the "cha gio" - also known as the spring roll - is a very popular dish to Vietnamese people.* Cha Gio *(cha:dzio:) can be made by most Vietnamese housewives. Its connoisseurs have ranged from the kings in ancient Vietnam down to the modern Vietnamese man-in-the-street. But it is a dish for Vietnamese receptions or parties, and not for daily meals because a good deal of time and toil is needed to make it.*

*The recipe below for* cha gio *has been written by Mrs. Le Hang Phan, a well-known instructor of the Vietnamese culinary art in the Washington area.*

## WRAPPING

2 lbs. of large rice paper
(for making about 24 large rolls)

## INGREDIENTS

MEATS
- 2 lbs. of ground fresh pork butt and fresh crab meat
- 2 eggs
All seasoned with:
- 2 teaspoons of gluctamate accent
- 2 teaspoons of nuoc mam (fish sauce)
- 1/2 teaspoon of ground pepper, either black or white
- 1/2 teaspoon of salt
Mix the whole combination
Cover and refrigerate

---

[1]*The above supplementary material is extracted from "Vietnam Times," February-March 1985 issue. It has been partially re-edited for inclusion in this study with the permission of the publisher of the magazine and the author of the article.*

VEGETABLES
- 1/2 lb. of finely chopped onions
- 1/2 lb. of grated carrots
- 1/4 oz. of Chinese dried mushrooms (tung-koo) soaked in water, then drained and sliced.
- 1/4 oz. of dehydrated wood fungus, also soaked in water then drained and sliced.
- 4 oz. of Chinese mung bean vermicelli softened in water, drained, then cut with scissors to about 3 inches long.

Take the meat mixture out of the refrigerator, and place it in a large bowl. Mix well. Next, mix the vegetables thoroughly and add them to the meat.

With a tablespoon, scoop that mixture onto a large plate to make about 24 meat balls.

HOW TO WRAP

Make a solution of 4 cups of water and 2 teaspoons of sugar; use a deep large plate to contain this sugared water.

Take one single sheet of rice paper at a time and dip it into the sugared water. Quickly take it out and let it drip off all excess water. Then lay it flat onto a large chopping board.

Take one of the meat balls, spread it on the softened rice paper. Shape it about 4 inches long and roll it the way you would roll a cigar but with both ends closed by folding the rice paper while rolling.

Do not arrange the rolls one on top of the other, but rather lay them separately onto a rack in your refrigerator overnight. This allows the rolls to dry out, and makes them easier to fry; it also makes them crispier. The sugared water helps them to get a beautiful golden brownish tint when fried.

## HOW TO FRY

Deep-fry the rolls in hot corn oil about 2 minutes on high heat, then 8 minutes on medium heat for the meat to cook, and finally the 2 last minutes on high heat again.

Be sure to turn the rolls over when one side looks done so that they cook evenly. Also when frying, never leave the egg-rolls unattended for they may get overdone.

Serve hot and crisp, along with Boston lettuce, various Vietnamese mints, and diluted nuoc mam (fish sauce).

## HOW TO PREPARE THE "NUOC MAM"

Make a mixture of the following:

- 1/4 cup of nuoc mam of famed brands
- 1/4 cup of white vinegar
- 3/4 cup of water
- 1/8 cup of sugar
- 2 cloves of fresh garlic, mashed
- some red hot pepper (optional)

Cha Gio can be frozen, either pre-cooked or raw. The rolls can be kept in a freezer for several weeks. Reheat them in the oven if precooked. Fry them if uncooked; but do not thaw! Fry them as soon as you can separate them, and do not crowd the pan, for the oil may get cold, and the rolls get too soft to fry and become crisp.

# 'ANGEL OF DEATH' ENDS DREAM
## Viet Grocer Slain Where He Sought
## The "Good Life"

By JOHN WHITMIRE
Post Reporter
The Houston Post, Thurs. March 14, 1985

Two weeks ago, a Vietnamese grocer told his wife he wanted to open more stores so he could give his children the "good American life."

About an hour later a good American customer — "The Angel of Death" — shot him to death, his grieving widow said Wednesday.

Bruce Wayne Coleman, 31, of the 5900 block of Selinsky, was charged with capital murder Tuesday in the Feb. 27 slaying-robbery of Long Thanh Tran. Houston homicide detectives said Coleman, who remained behind bars Wednesday without bond, claims to have shot the refugee in self-defense.

Police say Tran, 36, was alone in the small corner grocery store in the 3400 block of Dowling when a gunman came in about 10 p.m. and demanded money.

Tran was found sprawled in a pool of blood behind an emptied cash register. The next day, he died.

Tran's widow, Thuy Nguyen, said she spoke to her husband on the phone a short time before he was shot.

"He called me and talked about the many stores he wanted to buy in the future. He talked about taking some food home for the children," she said.

Nguyen, 33, said she is terrified that she may meet the same bloody fate.

"I am very scared, I was not scared before my husband was killed, but now I am very scared," she said in broken English. "If something happens to me, there would be nobody there to take care of my children."

Nguyen said she wants to sell the store they purchased last January because she doesn't have the time to run the business and raise her two daughters and three sons. They range in age from 8 to 14.

She said she fears she may have to sell the house they bought only three months ago. She said she doesn't think she can afford the $760-a-month mortgage.

Nguyen said she knew the man who has admitted killing her husband for about a year.

"My husband knew him a long time, too. He came in to this store to buy food, everything."

"He look dangerous. I saw it in his eyes. He look like an Angel, Angel of Death," she said.

Wallace Huntsberry Jr., like many neighbors, mourns the loss of his friend.

"He was the best in the world to me. He was overeasy to get along with. He'd always give people some credit, if they didn't have enough money. I've seen him catch people - children - stealing, and he'd let them go and let them have it (what they tried to steal)," said Huntsberry.

Huntsberry said he was in the store just a short time before Tran was slain.

"He was in his same old jolly mood. He called me friend. He called everybody friend. He had a lot of friends here, in this area."

Nguyen said her husband had always been a peaceful and friendly man, even when rockets and bullets flew over their small home on the coast of Vietnam.

She said the couple grew up together in a small fishing village. They married in 1968, and eked out an existence fishing.

But the war was going badly, and the couple finally decided to flee in 1975. With the Communists on their heels, the couple took 50 friends and set sail on their rickety boat.

They drifted aimlessly for days until they saw a U.S. Navy ship on the horizon. It was packed with refugees. They clambered on board, and set their small vessel adrift.

The ship sailed to Guam. Tran and Nguyen spent three months in cramped quarters filling out reams of paperwork in order to become American citizens.

From there, they were transported to Fort Chaffee, Ark., where they waited for another six months.

Finally, they were allowed to leave. Tran found a job making auto parts in a factory in Beaumont. About 18 months later, the family packed up their few belongings and moved to Illinois to be with Nguyen's mother. But there were no jobs up north, so they returned to Texas.

Tran netted a job as a fisherman in Port Arthur. It was a good job, but the family wanted more out of life, so they moved to the big city, Houston, in hopes of finding their dream.

He took a job in a can company, and she took a job making furniture. Their jobs paid little more than minimum wage, and the pair had five growing children to support.

They sat down and talked one day, and decided to open up a little grocery store. Tran liked the location of the store on Dowling, and so did his wife.

Said Nguyen, "But, right now, I am very sad. When I look at my children, I am very sad."

*(Reproduced with courtesy of Houston Post, Houston, Texas)*

# REFUGEE AGRICULTURAL PROJECTS: A FINANCIAL ANALYSIS
by Lawrence Pauling
The Bridge
Jan-Mar 1985

Agricultural development projects for Southeast Asian refugees are commonly characterized by policy-makers and program administrators as expensive and inefficient. This notion is based upon such project's cost per participant, which tends to be high. Yet, focusing on that cost is an inadequate way of judging whether agricultural training projects are worthy investments.

Refugee program policy-makers often fail to look at the following when assessing projects: benefit-cost analysis, net present worth, and internal rate of return. All three involve discounting the flow of benefits and cost of the project to "present worth". This type of analysis provides a framework within which financial and economic components of a proposed project can be evaluated, and it can point out the best use of resources, identify unrealistic or questionable assumptions, and indicate ways of which a project can be improved. (1)

### An Example of a Training Project

To demonstrate these methods, a hypothetical agricultural training project is presented below based on the author's personal experience with actual farm training projects for Southeast Asian refugees.

This project has a $265,000 budget to train 100 refugee heads of households (participants) over a period of 16 months. The extent to which 60 participants achieve "self sufficiency", or, for example, are off welfare by the end of training. The cost per participant is $2,650; if only 60 participants successfully complete training the cost per participant rises to $4,416. For the purpose of analysis, it is assumed that an equal amount of funding is available and utilized by the project each month. In the first year of training, the investment equals $198,750; in the remaining four months of training of the second year, the investment is $66,250. This budget covers the cost of 1 acre of production per participant during the entire training period, which includes summer and winter.

Benefits of the project include $50,000 in grant generated income from summer produce sales in the first year, and $10,000 from winter produce sales in the second year. On a per acre basis, these amounts break down as $500 and $200 respectively. All of the proceeds are retained by the project (or production cooperative) for future training. The other major stream of benefits that must be included in the analysis comes from the savings in welfare benefit payments. It is assumed that the average cash and in-kind payment for each participant (head of household), is equivalent to $1,200 a month for 13 years, and $600 a month for another 10 year period. These figures represent the public savings or the flow of benefits derived from training.

Table 1. Benefit-Cost Computations Comparing Net Benefit with Investment plus Operation and Maintenance Costs for a Refugee Agricultural Training Project with Three Participants Achieving Self-sufficiency.

| Year | Capital Items | Operations & Maintenance | Total | 10% Discount Factor | Present Worth | 1 (Gross Benefit) | Incremental Production Cost | 2 Cash Flow | 3 Net Value | 10% Discount Factor | 10% Present Worth |
|---|---|---|---|---|---|---|---|---|---|---|---|
| 1 | 198,750 | 0 | 198,750 | .9090 | 180,664 | 7,500[4] | 0 | -168,164 | 7,500 | .9090 | 6,817 |
| 2 | 66,250 | 0 | 66,250 | .8264 | 54,749 | 3,000[5] | 0 | -51,749 | 31,800 | .8264 | 26,280 |
| 3-15 | 0 | 0 | 0 | - | 0 | 518,400 | 0 | 518,400 | 43,200 | 5.8705 | 253,607 |
| 16-25 | 0 | 0 | 0 | - | 0 | 216,000 | 0 | 216,000 | 21,600 | 1.4709 | 31,771 |
| Total | 265,000 | 0 | 265,000 | - | 235,413 | 744,900 | 0 | 514,487 | 104,100 | - | 318,475 |

Benefit-cost ratio at 10% = 318,475/235,413 = 1.35

Net present worth at 10% = 318,475-235,413 = 83,062

1) Value of incremental production or gross benefit from production
2) Incremental net benefit
3) Net value of incremental production plus savings from welfare benefits
4) grant generated income: $2,500 per successful participant (from summer crop)
5) grant generated income: ≤1,000 per successful participant (from winter crop)

*Table 2*. Benefit-Cost Computations Comparing Net Benefits with Investment under two conditions of self-sufficiency: lifetime and one year.

| Situation | Benefit-Cost Ratio | ($)<br>Present Worth |
|---|---|---|
| 2 participants<br>(off-welfare for life) | .90 | -23,095 |
| 3 participants<br>(off-welfare for life) | 1.35 | 83,062 |
| 60 participants<br>(off-welfare for 1 year) | 3.08 | 489,201 |
| 30 participants<br>(off-welfare for 1 year) | 1.54 | 126,891 |

**Benefit-Cost Analysis**

Table I revelas the benefit cost computations of comparing net benefits with the project investment (costs) when 3 participants achieve self-sufficiency. This is the ratio obtained when the present worth of the benefit stream (savings of cash and in-kind benefit payments plus grant generated income) is divided by the present worth of the cost stream (project investment). The discount factor for analysis is placed at the generally prevailing interest rate of 10%. If the benefit cost ratio is less than 1, then the present worth of the benefits, and the initial expenditure cannot be fully recovered. In other words, if the benefit-cost ratio is 1 or greater, a positive return of investment results. In general, the higher the ratio, the greater the return on investment. The most common criteria for project funding is a benefit/cost ratio of one or greater.

As illustrated in the Table 2, if only three heads of households (3% of project participants) become self-sufficient for the remainder of their lifetime after training, the benefit-cost ratio is 1.35. This figure exceeds our acceptance criteria for funding. In fact, cost could rise 35% or benefits drop 30% before the benefit-cost ratio is driven down to one. If just two participants became self-sufficient, then the benefit-cost ratio would be .90, just slightly below the investment break-even point.

If a project were able to reach its employment target of 60 "heads of household" (Table 2), the benefit-cost ratio within one year alone would be an astonishing 3.08. In fact, with 60 participants off welfare, it would take less than 3.5 months to recapture the project invesment. If only 30 participants got off welfare (half the number of the project's objectives), the benefit cost ratio would be 1.54, still within the range of acceptance. Thus, the results indicate that within a few months, or with very few participants achieving self-sufficiency, the cost of the training project can be easily recaptured.

## Net Present Worth

The net present worth is the difference between the present value of the project's stream of benefit and costs. In the case of 3 participants achieving self-sufficiency for live, the net present worth of the project has generated a savings for taxpayers worth $83,062. if just two participants achieve self-sufficiency for life, then the net present worth of the project is $23,095. However, if 60 participants achieve self-sufficiency for just one year, the project generates a tax savings of $489,201; for 80 participants, the tax savings is $126,891.

## Internal Rate of Return

Another way of using the net benefit streams is to find the discount rate that makes the net present worth of the incremental cash flow equal to zero (2). This discount rate is called the internal rate of return. It is the maximum interest that a project would pay for resources to recover its investment. This measure is commonly used by the World Bank (and most other international financing agencies) for its economic and financial analysis of projects. Calculations for 3 participants gaining self-sufficiency for a lifetime reveals an internal rate of return of slightly less than 15%. This rate of return on resources invested in the project is approximately 5% higher than what would be achieved in capital markets at a 10% interest rate. As the benefit-cost ration increases, it can be expected that the internal rate of return will also rise.

## Viable Pursuits

From this brief analysis, we can see that the return of investment in refugee agricultural projects can be fairly high even at a very modest rate of successful completion. If agricultural projects cannot achieve a mere 3% success rate (3 out of 100 participants), or provide adequate skills for self-sufficiency for just a few months, then perhaps we need to investigate other reasons for this failure.

The real problem may lie with the way funds are administered. the way project goals are implemented, or even in the commitment of clients to become self-sufficient. In any case, this study demonstrates that agricultural projects are not wasteful, but viable financial pursuits and feasible economic ventures which benefit refugees and society alike.

*Lawrence Pauling is a consultant who has worked on refugee agricultural training projects in California for the Office of Refugee Services, the Stockton Farmers Cooperative, and Catholic Charities. He is currently working with the Hmong Highlander Development Fund at IRAC.*

°*Gittinger, J: Economic Analysis of Agricultural Projects,* 2nd edition, Johns Hopkins University Press, 1982.
²Ibid.
*(Reproduced with permission of the author and courtesy of "The Bridge" published by IRAC.)*

# ON CONFUCIANISM, TAOISM
# and BUDDHISM
## Nguyen Cao Thanh

For more than two thousand years, Asia has been deeply influenced by these great doctrines or religions: Confucianism, Taoism and Buddhism that have shown the way or Tao, the knowledge and proper maintenance of which undoubtedly lead to harmony and peace.

All these three philosophies or religions expound the Tao differently though they all would aspire to the same goal of imparting happiness to the suffering mankind.

Confucianism is based on the Four Books and Five Classics. With these holy scriptures which represent the written cultural heritage of ancient China, Confucius evolved the doctrine of jen (human-heartedness), the natural compassion of human heart with the ideal of human conduct as devotion to one's ancestors, family and nation.

While attacking great importance to man's life in this world and not his eternal life in the other world, Confucius expressed in simple terms his principle:

"I should like to bring security to the aged, to be loyal to my friends, and to be affectionate with the young."

Democracy was upheld both in fact and in spirit. The position of the people was even placed above the sovereign which meant the security and welfare of the nation should never be neglected. This fact was illustrated by Mencius:

"The people are the most important element in a nation; the spirits of the land and grain are the next; the sovereign is the lightest."

In the Book of Changes, the origin of the universe was discussed. It was the chaos at the beginning from which emerged the Tai Chi, the Supreme Ultimate which, through movement, produces the *Yang*. Having reached its limit, this movement is followed by quiescence, and by this quiescence, it produces the *Yin*.

By the transformation of the Yang and the union therewith of the Yin, Five Vital Elements are produced and distributed in harmonious order with the four seasons proceeding in their course.

Being human-centered rather than other-worldly, Confucius laid great emphasis on personal cultivation:

"From the Son of Heaven (the Emperor) down to the common people, all must consider the cultivation of one's own self as the root," bearing in mind five cardinal virtues: compassion, righteousness, propriety, wisdom and reliability.

While Confucius regarded Tao as the standard of ethics in human affairs, Lao Tze considered it as something analogous to the course of nature.

A work of great philosophical depth, the Tao Te Ching (Classic of the Way of Virtue) deals with the nature of the universe and of man.

Considering the human body as the cosmos in miniature, Taoism also advocates a line of conduct in harmony with Tao, the natural order of the Universe. To live in accordance with the Taoist doctrine of wu-wei (no action contrary to nature) means to lead a life of naturalistic simplicity and calmness with the minimum of organization and regulation.

Reversing the usual scale of values, Taoism prefers the simplicity of rural life, considers all means of winning possessions and power as a way to alienate man from Tao and disparages book-learning as a departure from naturalness.

Living in harmony with Tao, man can empty his mind and rids himself of all prejudices and selfish ambitions.

Like Buddhism, Taoism also tries to point out to mankind the cause of suffering but in simpler terms of Lao-Tze:

"The reason I have great trouble is that I have a body; if I had none, what evil could befall me?"

Once man understands that his body is a source of suffering, he no longer demeans himself to do anything that may disturb his inner peace and lower his spiritual value.

Instead of advocating strength, Lao Tze praises weakness:

"The hard and the strong are the fellows of death; the supple and the weak are the fellows of life."

Meekness, humility, compassion and frugality are the precious qualities that Taoism extolled.

"The reason why the River and the Sea are able to be King of the hundred valleys is that they take the lower position. Hence they are able to reign over the hundred valleys."

The similar wise attitude was preached by Jesus Christ who promised that the meek "will inherit the earth," (Mathew 5.5)

Taoism depicts the strength of weakness in an imagery style:

"There is nothing weaker than water, but none is superior to it in overcoming the hard."

While the Confucian ideal was an upright man fulfilling his proper place in society and the goal of the Taoist was to arrive at doing nothing on purpose, the Buddhist moral ideal was freedom from sin and its attendant consequences - future reincarnation on earth.

The Buddhist canon consists of three collections known as Tripitaka or the three Baskets (the Three Treasures of Buddhism).

The Buddhist feels safe as long as he puts into practice the fourfold Noble Truths which are a revelation of the symptons of a man's illness, its causes, its healing and the way of gaining the cure.

These truths have given a hope of salvation to all living beings including wicked men, beasts or hungry demons because Buddha nature is not something that comes to an end. We never lose our Buddha-nature. All of us are capable of attaining wisdom and Buddhahood.

The Fourfold Noble Truth needs to be thoroughly understood and be patiently accepted.

- To know the fact of suffering and its nature;
- To know the source of suffering;
- To know the bliss derived from the end of suffering;
- And to know the Noble Eightfold Path that leads to the end of suffering: right view, right thought, right speech, right behaviour, right livelihood, right effort, right mindfulness and right concentration.

To follow this Path to a successful end, the Knowledge of the Four Viewpoints proves to be very helpful:

- To think of the impurity of the body;
- To consider the mind to be in constant state of flux;
- To think of the transiency of one's life, the egolessness and impermanence of all things which are all aggregates that sooner or later will break apart and be scattered;
- To think of the inevitable suffering resulting from the accumulation of world things.

The law of casuality and change governs all phenomenon with Karma as the resultant of spiritual forces generated by deeds (physical, oral and mental).

Depending upon the spiritual tendency of the Karma, it will survive the body after death to reincarnate in one of the six forms of existences. Karma does not mean Fate but rather the sum total of the deeds done in previous existences. All living beings are what they are as the result of their past deeds.

For release
July 13, 1984
Vol. 1, No. 19

# WAS THE ANTI-WAR MOVEMENT WRONG?

Michael Novak

During the spring and summer of 1967, I became active in the anti-war movement in California. With Rober McAfee Brown and Rabbi Heschel, I contributed to a book, *Vietnam: Crisis of Conscience,* that sold more than 100,000 copies. Later, I joined the board of Clergy and Laity Concerned about Vietnam.

But these days, when I hear congressmen warn about "the Lessons of Vietnam," my conscience twinges. I have come to think that the anti-war movement was wrong - at least that I was wrong - about Vietnam. We misinterpreted the facts. We are now implicated in the immense miseries of the people of Vietnam, South and North.

What is the lesson of Vietnam? The lesson is that Marxist forces concentrate their most important effort on propaganda and disinformation within the United States and Europe. The frontline was never on the battlefield; it was on the US homefront.

In recent years, the aging leaders of North Vietnam have begun publicly about how successfully they deceived us - not only Jane Fonda and others who honored Hanoi, but also all of us who tried hard to believe that Ho Chi Minh was really "the George Washington of Vietnam".

The North Vietnamese lied to us about the "civil war" in South Vietnam, about the National Liberation Front, about the Viet Cong - and we fell for it. The North Vietnamese now boast that from the first they held their infiltrators into South Vietnam under tight Marxist discipline. After the war, they have not scrupled to murder or to keep imprisoned the gullible South Vietnamese who joined the Front without being Marxists.

Far from being a civil war, the war in South Vietnam was from the first conceived by North Vietnam as the first stage of a Marxist war of aggression for dominance over all of Indochina, including Cambodia and Thailand. From very early stages, the plan was to build a base for Soviet power, as a counterweight to China. The huge Soviet naval and air bases in South Vietnam, which now threaten sea lanes and peoples of the region, were not an afterthought.

What most hurts my conscience, though, is not the dire strategic threat to other innocent peoples, but rather the painful sufferings of the Vietnamese, North and South. Marxism is a harsh master. The Gulag has been extended beyond the USSR to oppress another 58 million human beings.

International authorities report that the nutritional levels at which Vietnamese are today forced to live - in that once rich agricultural land, called then "the rice bowl" of the world - are so low that most Vietnamese lack sufficient energy to work a full eight-hour day.

Re-education camps keep scores of thousands in facilities often worse than the "tiger cages." Local spying and terror, indoctrination and suppression, have reached classic Marxist levels.

Thatis why, abandoning all they have attained for generations, more than two million Vietnamese have brought and bribed their way to risk death upon the treacherous seas. Of those who flee, a minimum of one in ten die.

Pirates halt many of the others. All their valuables are torn from them. On average, women who flee are raped five times. Some are dragged away in captivity by the pirates. Some are brutally mutilated.

Just last month, the distinguished Paul Hartling, a theologian who is the UN High Commissioner for Refugees, reported an average of 5,000 refugees a month still getting through the cordon of death, rape, plunder, and captivity. It is unknown how many small boats are wantonly sent to the bottom after lusts for murder, robbery and rape are sated.

By now, the casualties at sea exceeds the casualties of the long war. We in the anti-war movement said from 1966-1976 that we cared about the Vietnamese. Did we really? What accounts, then, for our lack of caring since 1976?

"The reports," Dr. Hartling says, "are the most horrifying I have seen." On April 2 a boat carrying 12 men and 3 women was attacked, the hands of the men bound with nylon ropes, the last human valuables of these poor people confiscated, the 3 women raped again and again, and then their boat rammed and sunk. Only one survivor lived to tell the tale.

It is late, very late, to say we were wrong. Never to say so would be unconscionable complicity.

*(Reproduced with permission of the author and courtesy of American Enterprise Institute for Public Policy Research)*

# BIBLIOGRAPHY

"A Collection of Papers in Vietnamese Culture," Indo-chinese Culture Center, Houston, Texas, 1981.

Kenneth J. Albert, editor-in-chief, "Handbook of Business Problem Solving," McGraw-Hill Book Company, New York, 1980.

Frank S. Budnick, Richard Mojena, Thomas E. Vollman, "Principles of Operations Research for Management," Richard D. Irwin, Inc., Homewood, Ill. 60430, 1977.

Albert Z. Carr, "Business as a Game," New American Library, Bergenfield, N.J., 1968.

Molly Joel Coye and Jon Livingston, ed., "China - Yesterday and Today," Bantan Books, Inc., Des Plaines, Ill. 60016, 1975.

Merle E. Dowd, "How to Earn a Fortune and Become Independent in Your Own Business," Parker Publishing Co., West Nyack, N.Y., 1971.

C. William Emory, editor, "Manager for Tomorrow," by the staff of Rohrer, Hibler & Replogle, Mentor Executive Library Book, The New American Library, New York, 1965.

Ronald R. Gist, "Marketing and Society," Holt, Rinehart and Winston, Inc., New York, 1971.

James Haskins, "The New Americans: Vietnamese Boat People," Enslow Publishers, Hillside, New Jersey 07205. 1980.

Robert D. Hay, "Introduction to Business," Holt, Rinehart and Winston, Inc., New York, 1968.

Robert L. Heilbroner & Lester C. Thurow, "The Economic Problems," 6th ed., Prentice-Hall, Englewood Cliffs, N.J., 1981.

Don Hellriegel and John W. Slocum, Jr., "Organizational Behavior," West Publishing Co., St. Paul, 1976.

Tyler G. Hicks, "How to Borrow Your Way to a Great Fortune," Parker Publishing Company, West Nyack, N.Y., 1970.

Tyler G. Hicks, "How to Build a Second-Income Fortune in Your Spare Time," Parker Publishing Company, West Nyack, N.Y., 1965.

Tran Trong Kim, "Việt Nam Sử Lược" (Outline of the Trần Trọng Kim, "Việt Nam Sử Lược" (Outline of the History of Vietnam), Ministry of Education, Republic of Vietnam, 1971.

Otto Kleppner, "Advertising Procedure," 6th ed., Englewood Cliffs, N.Y., Prentice-Hall, 1973.

John K. Leba, "The Vietnam Syndrome," Zieleks Company, Houston, Texas, 1981.

James, Legge, Jr., "The Four Books," Chinese-English (bilingual) version, Taipei, Taiwan, Republic of China.

Maekawa Makoto, "Boat People, Vietnamese Refugees in Japan," English tr. by Fr. Martin Clarke and Ngo Chi Dung, Tokyo, Japan, 1978.

Joseph L. Massie, "Essentials of Management," Prentice-Hall, Englewood Cliffs, N.J., 1971.

R. Charles Moyer, James P. McGuigan & William J. Kretlow, "Contemporary Financial Management," West Publishing Company, St. Paul, 1981.

John J. O'Connor, "A Chaplain Looks at Vietnam," The World Publishing Co., Cleveland, Ohio, 1968.

Ishwer C. Ojha, "Chinese Foreign Policy in an Age of Transition: The Diplomacy of Cultural Despair," Beacon Press, Cambridge, Mass., 1969.

Price E. Patton, "Free from Money Worries," Bantam Books, Inc., Des Plaines, Ill., 1956.

Report to the Congress, January 31, 1983, Refugee Resettlement Program, U.S. Department of Health and Human Services, Social Security Administration, Office of Refugee Resettlement.

R.R. Rosenberg and Harris Lewis, "Essential of Business Arithmetic," McGraw-Hill Book Company, New York, 1964.

"The Bridge," publication of the Indochina Resource Action Center (IRAC), Washington D.C., 20036.

1982 ECONOMIC CENSUSES, "Refugees-Parolees Admitted to the United States by Nationality and Fiscal Year," 1972-1980, U.S. Department of Commerce, Bureau of the Census.

BACKYARD WILDLIFE

# Woodpeckers

by Kari Schuetz

BELLWETHER MEDIA • MINNEAPOLIS, MN

323.0929

Note to Librarians, Teachers, and Parents:

**Blastoff! Readers** are carefully developed by literacy experts and combine standards-based content with developmentally appropriate text.

**Level 1** provides the most support through repetition of high-frequency words, light text, predictable sentence patterns, and strong visual support.

**Level 2** offers early readers a bit more challenge through varied simple sentences, increased text load, and less repetition of high-frequency words.

**Level 3** advances early-fluent readers toward fluency through increased text and concept load, less reliance on visuals, longer sentences, and more literary language.

**Level 4** builds reading stamina by providing more text per page, increased use of punctuation, greater variation in sentence patterns, and increasingly challenging vocabulary.

**Level 5** encourages children to move from "learning to read" to "reading to learn" by providing even more text, varied writing styles, and less familiar topics.

Whichever book is right for your reader, Blastoff! Readers are the perfect books to build confidence and encourage a love of reading that will last a lifetime!

This edition first published in 2012 by Bellwether Media, Inc.

No part of this publication may be reproduced in whole or in part without written permission of the publisher. For information regarding permission, write to Bellwether Media, Inc., Attention: Permissions Department, 5357 Penn Avenue South, Minneapolis, MN 55419.

Library of Congress Cataloging-in-Publication Data
Schuetz, Kari.
Woodpeckers / by Kari Schuetz.
  p. cm. – (Blastoff! Readers. Backyard wildlife)
Includes bibliographical references and index.
Summary: "Developed by literacy experts for students in kindergarten through grade three, this book introduces woodpeckers to young readers through leveled text and related photos"–Provided by publisher.
ISBN 978-1-60014-599-5 (hardcover : alk. paper)
1. Woodpeckers–Juvenile literature. I. Title.
QL696.P56S39 2011
598.7'2–dc22                           2011002925

Printed in the United States of America, North Mankato, MN.

080111     1187